SOMETIMES YOU JUST NEED A PEP TALK

Pep Talks To Remind You How Truly Unstoppable You Are

JAMIE BROCKHURST

COPYRIGHT

Copyright © 2024 Jamie Brockhurst. All rights reserved.

Published by Thrive By Thought and Jamie Brockhurst. No portion of this book may be reproduced or copied, either electronically or manually, without the express written consent of the copyright holder.

Instagram: @thrivebythought

THRIVE BY THOUGHT

DEDICATION

This book is dedicated to you, the one reading this right now. You are *sensational*, you just need reminding of it sometimes.

Contents

TAKE WHAT YOU NEED 14

PEP TALKS FOR PERSONAL GROWTH 15

DON'T BE SCARED OF A ROCKY PATH 16
YOU ARE EXACTLY WHERE YOU ARE SUPPOSED TO BE RIGHT NOW 17
ONE SIZE DOES NOT FIT ALL 18
WHO ARE YOU LIVING FOR? 19
DON'T BE SCARED TO WALK ALONE 20
YOU ARE SUPPOSED TO FAIL 21
DON'T FORCE IT 22
DON'T BELIEVE EVERYTHING YOU SEE 23
WHO CARES WHAT THEY THINK 24
TRUST THE TIMING OF YOUR LIFE 25
YOU HAVE TO CHOOSE YOURSELF 26
HARD WORK ALWAYS PAYS OFF 27
WHAT'S MEANT FOR YOU WILL ALWAYS BE YOURS 28
FOLLOW THE NUDGES 29
REMEMBER WHO YOU ARE DOING THIS FOR 30
DO THE THING THAT SCARES YOU 31
REMEMBER WHAT REALLY MATTERS 32
BE DISCIPLINED 33
YOU HAVE TO RESCUE YOURSELF 34
FAILURE ISN'T PERMANENT 35
BE TRUE TO YOURSELF 36
REINVENT YOURSELF WHENEVER YOU WANT 37
REJECTION ISN'T PERMANENT 38
LIFE WILL FORCE YOU TO GROW 39
YOUR TIMING WAS ALWAYS WILDLY OUT OF WHACK 40

SOMETIMES YOU JUST NEED A PEP TALK

WHAT ARE YOU MAKING THIS MEAN 41
SUCCESS IS NOT A DESTINATION 42
BE BRAVE ENOUGH TO WALK AWAY 43
NEVER LET COMPARISON STEAL YOUR PEACE 44
SILENCE THE NOISE 45
GET OUT OF YOUR OWN WAY 46
STOP DOUBTING YOURSELF 47
YOU DID NOT COME THIS FAR TO ONLY COME THIS FAR 48
SWING AND A MISS 49
YOU DON'T NEED OTHER PEOPLE TO BELIEVE IN YOU 50

PEP TALKS TO REMIND YOU OF YOUR GREATNESS 51

YOU ARE AMAZING 52
REMEMBER WHO YOU ARE 53
YOU ARE CAPABLE OF ANYTHING 54
IF ANYONE CAN DO IT, IT'S YOU 55
ONE IN A MILLION 56
YOU ARE DESTINED FOR GREATNESS 57
YOU ARE POWERFUL 58

PEP TALKS TO MOTIVATE YOU 59

YOU WERE MADE TO DO BIG THINGS 60
LIVE FULLY 61
NEVER SETTLE 62
DO THE THING 63
BETTER THAN YOU COULD HAVE IMAGINED 64
SO WHAT'S STOPPING YOU? 65
MAKE THIS YOUR YEAR 66
YOU CAN'T QUIT 67

SOMETIMES YOU JUST NEED A PEP TALK

BE RELENTLESS 68
NON-NEGOTIABLE PROGRESS 69
SEIZE THIS MOMENT 70
YOU CAN TRANSFORM YOUR WHOLE LIFE 71
IT'S NOT OVER YET 73
YOU HAVE TO OVERESTIMATE YOURSELF 74
IT'S NEVER TOO LATE TO DO WHAT YOU WANT 75
DON'T LET ANYONE TRY AND STOP YOU 76
YOU ARE LIMITLESS 77
YOU ARE THE ONLY ONE WHO CAN CHANGE YOUR LIFE 78
PROVE THEM ALL WRONG 79
DON'T WASTE YOUR POTENTIAL 80
YOU GET TO DECIDE HOW THIS ENDS 81

PEP TALKS FOR WHEN YOU NEED TO TAKE IT UP A LEVEL 82

IT'S YOU VERSUS YOU 83
IF YOU ARE LOOKING FOR A SIGN THIS IS IT 84
TAKE IT UP A LEVEL 85
RAISE YOUR STANDARDS 86
WHAT WOULD THE BEST VERSION OF YOU DO 87
YOU ARE READY 88
BET ON YOURSELF 89
DECIDE 90
BECOME BULLETPROOF 91
NO MORE EXCUSES 92
RISE TO THE OCCASION 93
DON'T WAIT 94
REMEMBER WHERE YOU STARTED 95
LIFE IS ABOUT UPGRADES, NOT DOWNGRADES 96

SOMETIMES YOU JUST NEED A PEP TALK

THERE IS NO NEXT TIME	97
ASK FOR WHAT YOU WANT	98
100-YEAR-OLD YOU	99
LIFE GIVES YOU WHAT YOU ASK FOR	100
TREAT YOUR LIFE LIKE AN ADVENTURE	101
WHAT DO YOU WANT?	102

PEP TALKS TO REASSURE YOU 103

JUST A LITTLE REMINDER	104
YOUR LIFE IS NOT SUPPOSED TO BE PERFECT	105
SOMETIMES LIFE LOOKS MESSIER THAN IT IS	106
YOU ARE NOT BEHIND	107
ZOOM OUT	108
YOU CAN START OVER WHENEVER YOU WANT	109
YOU ARE STRONGER THAN YOU THINK	110
REJECTION DOESN'T DEFINE YOU	111
SOMETIMES THINGS HAVE TO HAPPEN FIRST	112
YOU CAN'T MESS UP	113
GOOD THINGS HAPPEN TO YOU	114
REJECTION IS REDIRECTION	115
LOOK HOW FAR YOU HAVE COME	116
EVERYTHING WILL BE OK IN THE END	117
IT'S NOT AS BIG OF A DEAL AS YOU THINK	118
GIVE IT TIME	119
DON'T WORRY ABOUT THE FUTURE	120
ONE DAY IT WILL ALL MAKE SENSE	121
ALL ROADS LEAD TO THE RIGHT DESTINATION	122
NO ONE KNOWS WHAT THEY ARE DOING	123
YOU ARE SO CLOSE	124

NEW DOORS ARE ALWAYS OPENING 125

YOU ARE OK 126

I KNOW HOW IT ENDS FOR YOU 127

THERE IS ENOUGH ABUNDANCE TO GO AROUND 128

IT WILL BE WORTH IT IN THE END 129

YOU CAN HANDLE MORE THAN YOU THINK 130

IT WILL HAPPEN 131

PEOPLE LIKE YOU WAY MORE THAN YOU THINK 132

BE PATIENT 133

IT GETS EASIER AND IT IS WORTH IT 134

PROGRESS DOSEN'T ALWAYS LOOK LIKE PROGRESS 135

EVERY DAY IS A BLANK CANVAS 136

YOU ARE DOING BETTER THAN YOU THINK 137

YOUR TIME WILL COME 138

PROGRESS 139

ONE DAY YOU WILL BE GRATEFUL THAT YOU DIDN'T GET WHAT YOU WANTED ... 140

PEP TALKS TO BOOST YOUR SELF-ESTEEM 141

TALK TO YOURSELF 142

HAVE MAIN CHARACTER ENERGY IN YOUR LIFE 143

YOUR YOUNGER SELF WOULD BE SO PROUD OF YOU RIGHT NOW 144

YOU ARE NOT SUPPOSED TO BE PERFECT 145

TAKE UP SPACE 146

STOP TRYING TO FIT IN 147

YOU DO NOT NEED ANYONE ELSE'S APPROVAL 148

YOU ARE SELF-MADE 149

THERE IS NOTHING WRONG WITH YOU 150

ALWAYS BUILD YOURSELF UP 151

REMEMBER WHAT YOU BRING TO THE TABLE 152

NO ONE GETS TO DECIDE WHAT YOU ARE WORTH 153
YOU CAN BE CONFIDENT 154
STOP SHRINKING YOURSELF TO MAKE OTHER PEOPLE FEEL COMFORTABLE 155
DON'T BELIEVE EVERYTHING YOU THINK 156
YOUR WORTH IS NOT DICTATED BY YOUR ACCOMPLISHMENTS 157
DON'T ABSORB THE NEGATIVE 158
YOU HAVE TO BELIEVE IN YOURSELF 159

PEP TALKS FOR SELF-LOVE 160

SELF-LOVE IS UNCONDITIONAL 161
YOU SHOULD BE PROUD OF YOURSELF 162
VOWS 163
TREAT YOURSELF RIGHT 164
THE END OF SELF-SABOTAGE 165
FORGET PERFECT 166
TAKE A COMPLIMENT 167
REGARDLESS OF THE SEASON 168
BODY CONFIDENCE 169
KNOW YOUR WORTH 170
YOUR LIFE ISN'T SUPPOSED TO LOOK LIKE ANYONE ELSE'S 171
DON'T BE SO HARD ON YOURSELF 172
YOU ARE ENOUGH 173
DON'T COMPARE YOUR LIFE TO ANYONE ELSE'S 174
BELIEVE IN YOURSELF 175
FOCUS ON YOU 176
IT'S OK IF YOUR LIFE DOESN'T LOOK LIKE YOU EXPECTED IT TO 177

PEP TALKS TO GUIDE YOU THROUGH UNCERTAINTY 178

YOU WILL ALWAYS FIND YOUR WAY 179

SOMETIMES YOU JUST NEED A PEP TALK

SEE WHERE IT GOES	180
NO ONE SAID IT WOULD BE EASY	181
JUST TAKE IT ONE STEP AT A TIME	182
DO IT AFRAID	183
LET GO OF THE OUTCOME	184
LIFE NEVER GIVES YOU MORE THAN YOU CAN HANDLE	185
IF YOU FEEL STUCK	186
YOU HAVE TO TAKE THE RISK	187
TRUST YOUR GUT	188
YOU ARE NOT LOST	189
YOU CAN'T CONTROL EVERYTHING	190
YOU DON'T NEED TO FEAR UNCERTAINTY	191
WHAT'S THE WORST THAT CAN HAPPEN	192
YOU ARE BRAVER THAN THAT	193
SOMETIMES IT DOESN'T GO TO PLAN	194
FEAR IS GOING TO COST YOU	195
NO MATTER WHAT HAPPENS	196
IN THE MOMENTS OF DOUBT	197
YOU ARE GOING TO HAVE TO PIVOT	198

PEP TALKS FOR TOUGH TIMES **199**

YOU HAVE TO EXPERIENCE ALL OF IT	200
IT IS ALL GOING TO BE OK	201
WHEN YOU ARE FEELING LOW	202
YOU ARE UNBREAKABLE	203
FINISH WHAT YOU STARTED	204
IT IS JUST A BLIP	205
IT IS NEVER THE WORST-CASE SCENARIO	206
COMPARTMENTALIZE IT	207

SOMETIMES YOU JUST NEED A PEP TALK

DON'T BE SCARED OF THE CHALLENGE	208
YOU CAN SURVIVE ANYTHING	209
YOU ARE TOUGHER THAN ANYTHING LIFE THROWS AT YOU	210
SINK OR SWIM?	211
IT GETS BETTER	212
THE STRUGGLE LEADS TO THE WIN	213
GET BACK UP NO MATTER WHAT	214
LIFE ISN'T ALWAYS FAIR	215
THE CHALLENGE WILL BUILD YOU	216
BETTER DAYS ARE COMING	217
THE COMEBACK IS ALWAYS BIGGER THAN THE SETBACK	218
THIS DOES NOT DEFINE YOU	219
YOU CAN DO HARD THINGS	220

PEP TALKS FOR THE RELATIONSHIPS IN YOUR LIFE 221

DON'T LET THEM FIND YOU WHERE THEY LEFT YOU	222
SOME PEOPLE WILL NEVER BE WHO YOU NEED THEM TO BE	223
MIXED SIGNALS ARE CRYSTAL-CLEAR SIGNS	224
YOU CAN LIVE WITHOUT THEM	225
DON'T CHASE PEOPLE	226
YOU ARE NOT GOING TO BE ALONE FOREVER	227
NOT EVERYONE IS GOING TO LIKE YOU	228
YOU ARE NOT TOO MUCH	229
READ THE RED FLAGS	230
ANOTHER PERSON'S OPINION OF YOU IS NOT FACT	231
HEARTBROKEN BUT NOT BROKEN	232
YOU ARE NOT RESPONSIBLE FOR ANYONE ELSE	233
WHOLE REGARDLESS OF YOUR RELATIONSHIP STATUS	234
LET YOURSELF BE JUDGED BY OTHERS	235

SOMETIMES YOU JUST NEED A PEP TALK

LOVE EXISTS	236
YOU DESERVE BETTER	237
WHAT IT MEANS WHEN THEY DON'T TREAT YOU RIGHT	238
LOVE SHOULDN'T BE PAINFUL	239
YOU CAN'T CHANGE OTHER PEOPLE	240
LOVE IS NOT EARNED	241
STOP ACCEPTING THE BARE MINIMUM FROM OTHER PEOPLE	242
YOU OWE THEM NOTHING	243
THE PEOPLE IN YOUR LIFE WILL CHANGE	244
YOU NEVER NEEDED THEM	245
SOME FRIENDSHIPS WILL EXPIRE AND YOU NEED TO LET THEM	246
HATERS ARE GONNA HATE	247
LET GO OF PEOPLE WHO ARE NOT YOUR PEOPLE	248
DON'T ACCEPT LESS FROM OTHERS	249
WHAT'S IN IT FOR YOU?	250
CHOOSE PEOPLE WHO CHOOSE YOU	251

PEP TALKS FOR INNER PEACE — 252

TAKE A DEEP BREATH	253
DEAR OVERTHINKER	254
TURN THE PRESSURE DOWN	255
YOU GET TO DECIDE	256
MAKE PEACE WITH NOT KNOWING ALL THE ANSWERS	257
LET YOURSELF REST	258
SAY 'NO' MORE	259
YOU DO NOT NEED TO CARRY EVERYTHING	260
YOUR LIFE IS FULL OF CHAPTERS	261
IT'S NOT YOUR PROBLEM	262
YOU DON'T HAVE TO BE STRONG ALL THE TIME	263

SOMETIMES YOU JUST NEED A PEP TALK

REBUILD YOURSELF	264
YOU DON'T ALWAYS HAVE TO KEEP THE PEACE	265
THE GOAL	266
IF YOU ARE FEELING OVERWHELMED	267
LET GO OF WHAT DOESN'T SERVE YOU	268
NOTHING IS MORE IMPORTANT THAN PROTECTING YOUR INNER PEACE	269
STRESS LESS	270

PEP TALKS TO HELP YOU HEAL 271

YOU WILL HEAL	272
FORGIVE YOURSELF	273
DEAL WITH WHAT YOU NEED TO DEAL WITH	274
LET GO OF THE PAST	275
YOU ARE GROWING	276
LET YOURSELF ENJOY THE SLOWER SEASONS	277
PAUSE	278
MOVE ON TO BETTER THINGS	279
NEVER LOOK BACK	280
GROWTH IS HARD BUT IT IS SO WORTH IT	281
FIND OUT WHO YOU REALLY ARE	282
LET YOURSELF GROW	283
GO TO WAR WITH YOUR ANXIETY	284
HISTORY IS NOT REPEATING ITSELF	285
STOP GASLIGHTING YOURSELF	286

TAKE WHAT YOU NEED

My whole life I have given myself pep talks. Pep talks when I am nervous, pep talks when I fail, pep talks when I get rejected, pep talks when I am attempting something big. Pep talks when I need a boost, pep talks when I feel insecure, pep talks for when things are changing. Pep talks for *every* single challenge I have faced. Because I know that if anyone's going to make the most out of my life, it has to be me. *Pep talks have been my lifeline.* So here are my pep talks written down for you. The pep talks that have changed my life for the better and taken me to highs that I could only ever dream of. You don't need to read this book in order, flick through and take what you need, take the boost of confidence, take the reminder of how loved you are, take the motivational kick, take the blunt reality check, take the kind warm hug. *Whatever* it is, use this book to give yourself the pep talk that you need. Because sometimes you just need that little chat with yourself to remind you just how powerful you really are and how you can handle anything that comes your way.

You've got this,
Jamie

SOMETIMES YOU JUST NEED A PEP TALK

PEP TALKS FOR PERSONAL GROWTH

DON'T BE SCARED OF A ROCKY PATH

Don't be scared of taking the rocky path. Sometimes the best things in life are only achievable by taking the harder path, the challenging path, the one with lots of uncertainty. What lies ahead of you may look daunting and scary but don't forget that you *can* handle it all and that it *will* be worth it. When you come out the other side you will realize that although the path was rocky and the route wasn't straightforward, you were capable of all of it. Sometimes to get what we really want for our lives we need to push a little bit harder; we need to go against the herd and choose a path that is different to the one we expected to be taking. Don't be afraid of this, sometimes the harder path is the only way to get what you want.

YOU ARE EXACTLY WHERE YOU ARE SUPPOSED TO BE RIGHT NOW

It might not feel like it but know that you *are* exactly where you are supposed to be right now. You are not behind, rather, you are *perfectly* positioned in your journey. Your life is always heading in the right direction and it is impossible for you to be in the wrong place or point in your life. I know it doesn't always make sense, but where you are in every moment is where you are *supposed* to be. Every high, every low, every challenge, every victory is all part of what you need to experience in that moment in order to move forward. You can't always see the progress you are making because you are too close to the action. If you step back a little you will see that even though life had a different plan for you to what you expected, it was ultimately the best route for you. Know that even if the current outcome is not what you envisioned it will all fall into place eventually. You are exactly where you are supposed to be in life, trust the journey, it will all come good.

ONE SIZE DOES NOT FIT ALL

The golden rule of a happy life is this: *You have to do it your way*. There is no such thing as 'one size fits all', you have to carve out your *own* path even if it looks completely different to everyone else's. Stand out from the crowd and do not feel obliged to follow the herd if that is what it takes to live in a way that makes *you* happy. Stand completely alone if you have to. Because one size does *not* fit all and it is better to be the odd one out than to sacrifice what you truly want your life to look like. Your life is *far* too valuable to be wasted doing what someone else wants you to do. You have to live on your terms and do so unapologetically. There is no *one* correct way to do life, you are in fact, totally and completely free to do whatever you want with your life. So do exactly that, this is *your* show.

WHO ARE YOU LIVING FOR?

Ask yourself honestly, who are you living for? It is so easy to get sucked into the loop of worrying what other people think of you. Do they like you? Do they think you are good enough? Are you deemed worthy in their eyes? Before you know it, you are doing certain things and making certain choices for your life to make sure that the outside world approves. If you aren't careful, you'll end up consumed with the goal of making sure that everyone around you - *the people you like and even the people you don't* - are happy with your life choices and are accepting of you. In other words, you start living for other people. You need to take back control, the quest for approval is a slippery slope, so you have to check-in with yourself and question your motives. Why do you make the choices you do? Whose path are you following? Is this for you? Is this even what you want? Or actually, deep down are you trying to keep other people happy? Take back the reins. This is your life - make sure you are living for you.

DON'T BE SCARED TO WALK ALONE

Be brave enough to walk alone at points in life. Sometimes you have to do things *by* yourself *for* yourself. It's in these times that you need to remember that actually, you were all you ever needed. You don't need others to carry you, *you can carry yourself.* You don't need anybody else to make your life amazing, *that's something you can do for yourself.* You are only ever dependent on yourself and you are everything you will ever need. You have made it this far in life depending *only on yourself.* Don't be scared to walk alone, it's only through walking alone do you realize just how powerful you are.

YOU ARE SUPPOSED TO FAIL

The thing that we forget is that we are *supposed* to fail occasionally and should *embrace* when we do fail. Go ahead and fail, it won't hurt you at all. In fact, it might just be the thing that helps you succeed. The best lessons come from failure and often the greatest successes come as a direct result of failing too. But also, in order to fail at something it means that you are actually attempting something, it means you are taking a leap out of your comfort zone and reaching for better. Which is amazing. Most people are so scared of failing they don't even try. Failing means that you were one of the exceptional ones who got off the start line and actually gave it a shot. It is better to fail than not even attempt something at all. Failing is part of the process of doing big things. You have to challenge yourself with things that are slightly out of your reach and push your capabilities. But with that comes the reality that you are going to overstretch and fail a few times in the process. Each time you fail you learn how to do better, it shows you where your weaknesses are so that you can work on them and turn them into strengths. It forces you to get creative and challenge your limits. *Failure is a strength*. No failure is permanent, but the lessons you learn and the growth you obtain in the process are.

DON'T FORCE IT

Don't force it. Big decisions, meaningful moments, relationships, connection with others, friendships, trust, love and enjoyment. These things *can't* be forced. They should come naturally or *not at all*. It's normal to have to work on things, but if you need to force it then it's not meant to be and *that's ok*. You are more likely to get what you want in the long run if you *don't* force things. The resistance you feel when things are being forced is your sign that it's just not right and you could do better elsewhere. Listen to that, prioritize your long-term happiness and don't force it.

DON'T BELIEVE EVERYTHING YOU SEE

It is so easy to look around you and think that everyone else is doing so much better than you. Please don't believe everything that you see. We are all so conditioned to only show the best parts of our lives. We share the victories, the achievements, the perfect milestones and blissful moments. Everyone tells you when they are winning, but no one ever tells you when they are losing. So when you are watching these filtered showreels of other people's lives, don't forget that it is *not the full picture*. It has been carefully tailored to show the world only the good bits and leave out the bad. Don't be fooled by the smoke and mirrors. No one has it all together all the time, no one's life is perfect, and no one has all the answers. We all have our own complications and challenges going on, you do not know what people are dealing with behind closed doors. Understand that life will be messy for all of us at points and that no path is ever perfectly straight. Focus on *your* path and on making *your* world as magical as you can, *for you*. You are doing so much better than you think you are. Your life is incredible, and you can't let comparison make you think otherwise.

WHO CARES WHAT THEY THINK

Who cares what they think? Who cares if they like you? Who cares if they don't? You need to remember that someone's opinion of you does not actually affect your life in *any way*. If they don't want the best for you then they *simply don't count* and therefore neither do their opinions of you. You have to be selective as to who you really let matter to you in your world. Remember that it is a *privilege* to have access to your life. You can't care about what everyone thinks of you, it is exhausting and you have much more important things to be getting on with. People are always going to judge you because that's just what people do, everyone is going to have an opinion of you and you can't take each opinion personally. Focus on what *you* think of *yourself* - that's the opinion that *actually* matters. Stay focused on *your* progress, *your* priorities and *your* happiness. Nothing is more important than that.

TRUST THE TIMING OF YOUR LIFE

Have you ever found yourself looking at the people around you and feeling left behind? Like they are moving forward with goals and milestones, whilst you are still trying to find your way. Trust the timing of your life. It *will* happen for you; you are going to get what you want when the *time is right* and it's going to be *better* than what you imagined. The recipe for each of our lives is different and right now life is concocting the most extraordinary path for you, giving you everything you need and more. Life is always guiding you and looking at the bigger picture that you can't see. Look back on your life and recognize how many things have worked out amazingly for you, even if the timing did not match what you envisioned. Don't waste this part of your journey consumed with worry about things not happening. Things *will* fall into place and it's *all* on track, but you are going to miss out on this part of your life if you focus on what you *don't* have yet rather than what you *do*. You think that *you* have great plans for yourself, but life has bigger and better plans for you than you could *ever imagine*. You need to start trusting, it is all lining up for you.

YOU HAVE TO CHOOSE YOURSELF

This is your reminder that you *do have* to choose yourself and put *yourself* first sometimes. *You* are a priority and *your* needs do matter. But no one is going to come and do this for you, you have to step up for yourself. Choosing yourself means prioritizing what you think of *yourself* over what other people think of you. Choosing yourself means letting other people down in order to not let yourself down. Choosing yourself means saying no to things that don't work for you and embracing the things that do. Choosing yourself means no longer *negotiating* with your happiness and instead standing firm in what *you* need to be happy. Choosing yourself means working on your insecurities and challenging the fears and doubts that hold you back. Choosing yourself means doing the hard things because you will benefit from them in the long run. Choosing yourself *isn't always easy,* but you are worth every bit of that extra effort.

HARD WORK ALWAYS PAYS OFF

Hard work *always* pays off. You will never ever regret giving something your all, you will never regret going for it guns blazing and playing full out for the end goal. I know you may not feel like it, I know there may be a million things you would rather do right now, but I promise you that this period of hard work *will* be worth it. You won't need to work this hard forever, you just need to give it your best shot right now, because this is about planting the seeds for future success. Imagine the day when you have achieved what you want, when you can finally put your feet up and look back at what you created with the hard work that you put in. I know it isn't easy now, *but it's not about now.* It's about the bigger picture, that is why you are doing this. It will all be worth it in the end because hard work *always* pays off.

WHAT'S MEANT FOR YOU WILL ALWAYS BE YOURS

You can't ruin, mess up or miss out on something that is destined for you. What is destined for you is destined for *you* and *you* alone. Nothing can take it away. Understand that your chances of happiness are not as fragile as you think. You don't need to live in fear that one false move or one wrong decision will take away everything you have ever wanted. It's yours, it's got your name written all over it, it's safe and it will find you. Just as you are seeking it, *it will seek you.* Relax into the idea that your life is *incredible*, and that all the wonderful things that are meant for you are on their way and you cannot mess that up.

FOLLOW THE NUDGES

Know that you are *always* being guided and supported. Life will *nudge* you in the right direction to lead you to where you are meant to be. Often these nudges feel like discomfort in your life. Whenever you feel stuck, lost, unsettled or when things feel like they don't sit right anymore; *you are being nudged*. Life will nudge you to make you understand that it's time for you to take action in your life. It will nudge you if certain situations, people and places are no longer right for you. It will nudge you when you have outgrown something and it's time to move on. It will *force* you to recognize that you can do better and make you push for more. Everything you need to know in order to better your life is in the nudges. They force you to take action in your life by making it too *uncomfortable* to stay where you are. So often we think that discomfort in our life is a bad thing *but it's not*. Discomfort is actually a reminder that we deserve better and we need to *go and get better* for ourselves. Follow the nudges, they will show you the way.

REMEMBER WHO YOU ARE DOING THIS FOR

Your success is going to make some people uncomfortable. Not everyone in your life is going to like seeing you succeed or cheer for you when you need it most. When following your dreams you are going to face rejection, disapproval and unhelpful comments, even at times when what you *really* need is support. In those moments, you need to remember this: *You aren't doing this for them.* This was never about them, this was always for you. Yes, their support would be nice, but it was never a necessity. They were never the main motivation for getting your life focused. They were never your muse or your purpose. This was about doing what is right for **you**. Some people are still too busy fighting with their own issues and insecurities to be happy for you when you are winning, but you can't let that be the reason you hold yourself back. You have to keep progressing, *whether they like it or not.* This is your life and you have to choose yourself above anyone else every single day.

DO THE THING THAT SCARES YOU

You won't ever feel fearless, we are hardwired to have fears and so they never truly go away. But what you can do is change your perception of what you fear until it no longer has the same power over you. Fear is a perception and how we perceive things changes throughout our life. Almost all children are terrified of the dark, but when they become adults they are not. The dark didn't change, but the perception and in turn the fear of the dark has changed. You need to choose a new perspective regarding what it is that you fear. The best way to do that is to *do* the thing that scares you. Move *towards* what you fear. Because when you do that, you realize that all the terrifying outcomes you expected to happen *didn't happen*, they were all just in your head – and even if something challenging did happen you will realize that you *can* handle it. Once you face what you fear head-on, quickly you will realize it *never actually* had any power over you in the first place. Do the thing that scares you, you have nothing to lose.

REMEMBER WHAT REALLY MATTERS

Never forget that the main goal is to be happy, everything else is secondary. It can be so easy to get wrapped up in all the things in life that *feel* so big but don't *actually* matter. We have goals, strict deadlines, to-do lists and plenty of things we want to achieve. We get so lost in the stress of it all and then feel guilt, shame and inadequacy when we haven't done the abundance of things that we tell ourselves we *should* have done by now. But really, *none* of that matters unless we are happy. Nothing is more important than that. You get to live this life **once** and once only. Don't let yourself miss out on the joy of being alive because of trivial things like to-do lists and goals. They don't really matter in the grand scheme of it all. Do the small things that make you happy along the way and let yourself actually *enjoy* your journey.

BE DISCIPLINED

No one, and I mean absolutely no one, enjoys being disciplined or enjoys doing the hard stuff. But that's the point, it's not about enjoying it, it's about doing what you *need* to do in order to *get* what you want out of your life. *It is about the bigger picture.* Discipline is the small sacrifice you make for the big win of getting what you want. No one said it was going to be easy, it's not all fun and games. There will be points where you have to do things that you don't actually want to do at all, and that is why you need discipline. Discipline gets you where you want to go. So stop delaying your own progress, be disciplined and do what you need to do. Keep yourself in check and remember why you started. Because it *will* feel worth it when you create the life you want. That's why you are doing it, so that you can look back and one day say *'Wow that was all me, I really did that'*.

YOU HAVE TO RESCUE YOURSELF

At the end of the day, it all comes down to you and *you* alone. *You have to rescue yourself.* It is down to *you* to change things and improve your life. I know that when you are in the thick of it, all you want is someone to come and rescue you, to take away all of the pressure and to sort it all out. But that person doesn't exist and no one is coming, it's purely down to you. But actually that's alright. That's alright because that means it's *you* who gets to write the rest of your story. It is *you* who has the opportunity to make *anything* happen from this point forward. You are the one calling the shots, you are the one who gets to design how your life looks and feels. *You have the power.* You can rescue yourself from anything in life, and that happens the second you decide that *you* run your life and it is your responsibility and no one else's. Where you are now bears no reflection on where you could be in the future. Anything is possible from any starting point in your life, but it can only be done by *you*.

FAILURE ISN'T PERMANENT

Somewhere along the way you bought into the idea that failure would be the end of the world for you. That if you failed it would be devastating and so failure *must* be avoided at all costs. The truth is, you are more fearful of failure than you need to be. Failure scares you as you expect it to lead to the worst-case scenario. But if you really stop and think about it, even in the worst-case scenario you would figure out how to be fine. You would problem solve and do what you need to do to be okay. Worst-case scenario is never really the worst-case scenario. If it all fell apart because you had failed then all that would happen is you would get up, dust yourself off and get started again. You might be bruised but truthfully *you would be fine*. Because failure is never as powerful or as permanent as you think it is. Nothing can ever get to you the way you think it can. You're actually pretty safe in life and when things do go wrong you will bounce back better, no matter what happens. Failure can't end you, failure doesn't define you and no failure can last forever. You will recover and move on.

BE TRUE TO YOURSELF

Certain situations in life will cause you to feel like you need to change who you are or compromise your values in order to be accepted. They will make you think that standing out or being different is a bad thing. But you must stay true to yourself *no matter what.* Be unapologetically proud of everything that you are. Never sacrifice who you are for someone who can't accept you as you are *already*. The people and places that want you to change to suit them were never *your* people and places in the first place. That isn't where you belong. Staying in the wrong places will leave you feeling like *you* are the problem. You are not the problem, the company you keep is. Let people see the real you, the raw and unfiltered version. The version of you that is not trying to live up to anyone else's expectations but the version of you that is genuine all the way. Your happiness lies in your authenticity, so each time you compromise your authenticity you are chipping away at your happiness. Be true to yourself, no matter what.

REINVENT YOURSELF WHENEVER YOU WANT

You can change your life whenever you want, you can decide that this isn't working for you, and you can choose to reinvent yourself into a version *that does*. This is *your* life, and *you* get to decide the next evolution you make. Reinventing yourself and evolving throughout your life is essential because without that there is no growth. You can, whenever you want to, decide that it's time to grow. You can decide that you want to make changes, big or small and you can make those changes happen. Too often we limit ourselves and who we could be based on who we have been before. It doesn't matter who you are or have been previously, you can begin again and start over as a completely new version of yourself. Because that's the whole point. This is a re-invention of you, it's *supposed* to be completely different. Let yourself discover what it is that you really want from your life and make *that* happen. You have nothing to lose.

REJECTION ISN'T PERMANENT

So many people who have what you want were also rejected countless times. It was their refusal to accept the rejection as defeat which has made them who they are. See rejection for what it is, a temporary 'no' until you find your 'yes'. Know that the rejection you face today has no negative impact on your future success unless you *choose* to let it do so. You get to decide how this ends for you. This rejection isn't permanent, you will get up, try again, push through this and get to where you want to be.

LIFE WILL FORCE YOU TO GROW

Life will force you to grow. It will force you to make moves and do the things that you need to do for yourself but haven't done yet. When you are reluctant to take the next step life will *push you* to take the next step. Often, life will force you to grow by making you feel uncomfortable in your current circumstances. As though everything you're doing right now is just slightly off. It does this so you *have* to take action. You've been sitting still and not making changes, so it takes away the choice and pushes you to make changes so that you grow, expand and take your life to the next level. *Discomfort is a sign that it's time to grow.* So what you may think is a low point or a slump in your life is actually a **new beginning**. It is a rebirth and period of upgrade. You are being moved to a place where you can reach your full potential. Life will force you to grow, let it.

YOUR TIMING WAS ALWAYS WILDLY OUT OF WHACK

Your timing was always going to be wildly out of whack. Whatever time frames you set for all the many things you wanted to do with your life, your timing was always totally and utterly unrealistic. We all do this. We all *wildly* overestimate what we can do in a totally unrealistic amount of time. We all plan for the *perfect* outcome in the *ideal* time frame. But life isn't 'perfect' and things rarely follow the 'ideal' plan. So if you haven't achieved what you wanted to by now, give yourself a break. You haven't failed and it's not as bad as you think, you just got your timings wrong from the beginning. You are still on the right path, you still are doing *so* well and you are going to get to exactly where you want to go. Just at a different time to what you had in mind. A more realistic time. Because it doesn't really matter whether it happens today or at some point in the future, just so long as it happens, and it will.

WHAT ARE YOU MAKING THIS MEAN

Ask yourself, *'What am I making this mean?'*. How you perceive the world is *everything*. Every situation in life is neutral, it has no meaning. It is meaningless. It isn't good, it isn't bad, it just *is*. We as humans add meaning where there isn't any to help us make sense of the world. You have to be aware of the meaning that you add to things because that is how you shape your world. A job rejection doesn't mean you aren't good enough for the job. A breakup doesn't mean you are unlovable or undesirable. Failing at something doesn't make you a failure. These are all just meanings that you created. Everything is ultimately a matter of perspective, and you can either build your life up or tear yourself down depending on how you choose to view things and the meaning you add. You control that.

SUCCESS IS NOT A DESTINATION

We often think of success as the finish line, the end goal, the big finale. The point where you have finally ticked off all of the things that you dreamt of achieving. That is *not* what success is. Success is *not* a destination. Success lives in the little things that are often overlooked because we are too busy focusing on our next move. Success is laughing so hard that you are gasping for air. Success is sharing a moment with someone you love. Success is being brave enough to do what makes you happy. Success is remembering who you really are and not accepting less than you deserve. Success is saying 'no' when something doesn't work for you. Success is being kind to yourself when things are tough. Success is deciding to bet on yourself and take the risk. Success is knowing when to walk away. Success is every time you dig deep and leave your comfort zone. Success is liking yourself. Success is waking up and realizing that you have been given another day. Success is finding what makes you happy and doing more of it. So before you give yourself a hard time for not being successful enough, realize that you are measuring success all wrong. Success isn't a destination; it is thousands of daily moments that you are so blessed to have. Your life is already a *massive* success.

BE BRAVE ENOUGH TO WALK AWAY

Be brave enough to walk away anytime a place, person, situation, relationship, job or lifestyle is no longer in *your* best interest. Even if this is the hardest thing you ever do, always be brave enough to walk away and put your happiness first. You matter above all and if something is no longer right for you then you owe it to yourself to leave the situation. It can be so terrifying to leave something so familiar to you *even* if you know it's bad for you, but nothing is worse than staying somewhere that you no longer belong. Some things are just not meant to be and you can't force them to work by staying. It is ok to outgrow things, to realize that this isn't right for you anymore and that you can do better. But it is *not ok* to sacrifice your current and future happiness by settling for less than you deserve. That would be a betrayal to *yourself.* You have got to make hard decisions that benefit you overall and that takes bravery, but remember, you *are* brave. There is a future version of you that is *so* grateful that you were brave enough to walk away today and demand more for yourself. You know what you have got to do.

NEVER LET COMPARISON STEAL YOUR PEACE

Whatever it is you are looking for, you are not going to find it looking over at someone else's life. Comparison will take everything from you but give you nothing back in return. Know that you are exactly where you need to be right now, and you are enough *regardless* of what anyone else is doing. There is no one that you need to try and keep up with. It's *not* a race, it is *not* a competition and there is *no* first-place trophy at the end of it. You do not need to be doing anything in particular with your life right now. There is no rule book, no expectations and no right and wrong. Everyone is on their own journey and different things happen for different people at different points in their journey. Things will unfold perfectly at the perfect time for *you,* and your life is not supposed to look like anyone else's life. No two lives are the same, live your life in your own way and on your own time. It's not about what others are doing in their life, it is about being happy with your *own* life.

SILENCE THE NOISE

What happens when you silence all of the noise around you? When you turn the volume down on everyone else's wants, needs, expectations and demands of you, and instead listen to the small whisper deep inside you begging to be heard. You know what you want deep inside, you know what is right for you and you know what path you need to take - *but you aren't listening.* That part of you is being muted by everything around you. Slow yourself down and tune into the silence, strip back all the noise and interference from everyone else around you so that you can finally actually hear *yourself.* Make *your* voice the loudest voice in your life and ask yourself *'What is my next move?', 'What is right for me?', 'What is going to make me happy?'* and then *actually* listen to what comes up for you. You have to live in a way that is authentic to you, regardless of what anyone else thinks of it. Because if you aren't living for yourself, you aren't *really* living at all.

GET OUT OF YOUR OWN WAY

Get out of your own way. No more excuses, no more self-doubt and no more giving yourself a hard time. Because the things you think are stopping you are not *really* stopping you. Get out of your own head, stop overthinking things and just *get on* with whatever you want to do. It's easy to blame outside factors, but at the end of the day, it is you versus you. It is the battle between the version of you who wants to go out there and live life to the fullest and the version of you that listens to the fear. You have to decide which version you are going to give power to. If you really want your life to change you have to get out of your own way.

STOP DOUBTING YOURSELF

Stop doubting yourself. You've got this, you can do anything that you put your mind to. But if you keep telling yourself you *aren't ready* or you *can't do it,* then that is exactly what you are going to believe. Doubt grows when you feed it so you need to *stop* giving it your energy. When you feel a flicker of doubt come up, crush it. Stop it growing straight away and don't let it start to feel real. You are going to believe everything that you tell yourself, so stop filling your mind with thoughts that hold you back. *You* run your mind, remember that. Remind yourself of how incredible you are, how capable and how worthy. *Force* confidence upon yourself until you feel confident. The word *force* is the key thing - you aren't going to want to fight your doubt, but you absolutely have to. Get those reigns back, this is *your* life.

YOU DID NOT COME THIS FAR TO ONLY COME THIS FAR

Don't stop now. *I mean it.* You can't stop now. You did not come this far to *only* come this far. You have been through hell and back to get here. Every setback, every challenge, every obstacle that you overcame brought you to this moment. You fought for this moment with everything you had. Throughout the years you have seen so much, achieved so much, conquered so much and overcome so much. You outdid every single person's expectations of you. Time and time again you dug deep and showed the most incredible strength in the face of obstacles. So as you sit here today, remind yourself that you didn't come this far to only come this far. You aren't finished yet, you didn't overcome everything just to finish here. This is just the beginning for you, and you cannot settle for anything less than the absolute best for yourself. Deep down you know that there is so much more that you need to achieve and conquer, so finish what you started.

SWING AND A MISS

Don't be scared to take a swing, just in case you miss. You're not supposed to get it right all the time. You are going to make mistakes and you are going to fail and that is *absolutely* ok. Don't be scared of failing. Failure doesn't have as much power over you as you think it does and you can't let failure stop you from trying. If it matters to you, you've *got to* take a swing at it. Give it everything you've got and go in expecting a great outcome, and if you fail, so what? It's *ok* to fail, but it's not ok not to try. You have to always be moving forward and if that involves failing a few times then so be it. Everyone fails at some point, it's not a big deal. Getting back up is what matters, promise yourself that you will *always* get up and recover from anything. Promise that you will try again and again with zero judgment of yourself. Don't make failure personal, it's not. Take the swing, you have nothing to lose but everything to gain.

YOU DON'T NEED OTHER PEOPLE TO BELIEVE IN YOU

You don't need other people to believe in you for you to believe in yourself. What they think you are capable of has nothing to do with what you are *actually* capable of. The only person who needs to believe in you is *you*. The only person who can control the outcome is *you*. But if you keep listening to what other people think of you then you are never going to get off the start line. People are going to doubt you, that is just how it goes. The biggest mistake you can make is thinking that their opinion of you actually carries any weight. Only you know what you are capable of. They don't know the lengths you will go to succeed. Never forget that your life is worth *so much more* than someone else's opinion of you. Tune out the noise and go and prove them wrong.

PEP TALKS TO REMIND YOU OF YOUR GREATNESS

YOU ARE AMAZING

You need to know this: No matter how you feel right now, it doesn't change the fact that you are truly amazing. You are incredible, worthy and you deserve *the best*. You are doing great; I know it can be hard sometimes but you really are doing an amazing job. You owe it to yourself to feel good about yourself. You are totally and utterly amazing and the world is a better place because you exist. The issue is, you sometimes forget all that and think less of yourself than you should. Don't let your mind play tricks on you and make you think you are not enough when really *you are everything*. Never forget that.

REMEMBER WHO YOU ARE

Do not, not even for a second, forget how damn incredible you are. You are outstanding, one-of-a-kind, brave and brilliant. You are resilient and fierce, and you have *always* been in a league of your own. You have that something special about you that is solely *yours* and that no one else can replicate. So *remember who you are* and remember what you are capable of. This life has something big in store for you and you aren't going to let that pass you by. You were made for great things, and you *will* get where you want to go. You are one in a million, and if you just reminded yourself of that you could *quite literally* set the world on fire. So dust yourself off, take a deep breath and remember who the hell you really are and what you came here to do. You are not finished yet.

YOU ARE CAPABLE OF ANYTHING

You are capable of *anything*. Burn that sentence into your brain - '*I am capable of anything*'. Set it as your wallpaper, chant it in the shower, paint it on the side of your house and get it tattooed on your left bum cheek if you have to. *Whatever* it takes for you to stop believing your made-up excuses as to why you *can't* and instead start seeing that there is absolutely nothing stopping you, *and there never wa*s.

IF ANYONE CAN DO IT, IT'S YOU

Do not doubt yourself - not even for a second. You can do anything. No questioning it, no maybes, without a shadow of a doubt, if anyone can do it - *it's you*. You are capable of *anything*. You were built differently, you are not like anyone else. No one can compare to you, and it is *you* who can take on the world and make something spectacular out of it. You are so much more capable than you realize, and you owe it to yourself to give it everything you've got. You know you can do this, you know that you can beat the odds and win. This victory is yours, it's almost like your whole life has led up to this moment. Maybe that's exactly what has happened, everything so far has led you to this moment because this win was *always* meant to be yours. So rise to the occasion and give it everything you have got. Because if anyone can do this it is you.

ONE IN A MILLION

You are one in a million. Quite literally one of a kind and no one can compete with that. You are phenomenal and your life is phenomenal. So isn't it time that you started believing it too? Walk out into the world with your head held high, knowing to your very core that you are incredible. There is no one quite like you, and that is your superpower. Nobody can compare to you and nobody can be you. You are not a carbon copy, you are an original masterpiece. So start acting like it. Start making the most of everything that you are, the quirks, the strengths and the beautiful imperfections that make you different. Start seeing your life as truly remarkable, *because it is*.

YOU ARE DESTINED FOR GREATNESS

You are destined for greatness. The path ahead of you is *extraordinary* and nothing is going to stop you from doing amazing things. Deep inside, you have always known that you have something special about you, something that makes you stand out head and shoulders above the rest. You have always known that you were meant for more and that you were destined to do great things. Embrace *every* part of that, push for the very best for yourself and chase your dreams. You are nothing short of extraordinary.

YOU ARE POWERFUL

Do not forget just how damn powerful you are. Life has dealt you a few blows and it has made you doubt yourself and forget just how powerful you are. That's understandable, but that ends *here*. Going forward you are going to remember how capable you are, how extraordinary you are and how much *you matter*. You are going to fully step into your power and embrace everything that you are. No more holding yourself back. No more doubting yourself or fearing your potential. You are going to go out there guns blazing and live the life that you really want. You are going to reach your *full* potential and you are going to take action and make moves to change your life for the better. You are going to prioritize yourself and your needs and you are never going to shrink yourself again. No more hiding. No more quitting on yourself. Get it together and start seeing yourself for *all* that you are worth.

PEP TALKS TO MOTIVATE YOU

YOU WERE MADE TO DO BIG THINGS

You only get this *one* life, this *one* chance to do everything that you want to do. You can't afford to waste it by holding back and listening to your fears. You owe yourself more than that. You owe yourself a real opportunity to go hard and see what you are capable of. *Go big* and get what you want from your life. You have *never* wanted small for yourself, you know that you were made to do big things. You have always had that feeling inside you that you were made for *more* and you *have* to listen to that. So take a *real* shot on yourself, set huge goals, take action, make massive moves and push for more. You have nothing to lose and *everything* to gain. Take your one chance and go big, even if it scares you to do so. Stretch your limits and really see what you are made of because *that's* where the magic happens.

LIVE FULLY

Shoot your shot *every* single time. Speak up when you want something. Be in the moment. Don't waste time worrying. Let yourself feel good things *deeply*. Say I love you with no fear or expectations. Book that flight and take that trip. Do the things that scare you. Don't take anything too seriously. Know that whatever it is it can always be fixed. Laugh *constantly*. Fear nothing. Put yourself first. Chase your dreams. Expect incredible things to happen for you. Take calculated risks. Ask for what you want. Push your luck. Appreciate that your life is precious. Never sweat the small stuff. And always, *always* order dessert.

NEVER SETTLE

Never settle. Make that a rule that you live by. You settle when you are scared. You settle when you fear that life won't give you more, so it feels safer to settle rather than take the risk. If deep in your soul you know that you deserve better than what you are accepting, *then you are settling*. By settling you are not even giving yourself a chance to see what life has waiting for you right around that corner. Life will *always* provide. Everything that you want is out there waiting for you, praying that you don't settle and give up before you have a chance to reach it. Chase after what you want in its *full* glory. Decide that you deserve better than *'just ok'*. It may be a challenge to get there, but all the best things in life are worth that little bit of extra effort. You were not put on this earth to live half-heartedly. Settle for what you *actually* want, never settle for less.

DO THE THING

Do the *thing* you can't stop thinking about. The *thing* that you daydream about as you sip your morning coffee, the same *thing* that your mind wanders to as you fall asleep each night. Do the *thing* that lights you up every single time you think of it. The *thing* that makes you feel alive. Do the *thing* that makes you envious when you see other people doing it. The *thing* that you have wanted for as far back as you can remember - it's *your thing*. It always has been and it always will be. Do the thing because if you don't do the *thing,* you will *always* be wanting to and wondering what if? That kind of pull doesn't go away on its own. It's an itch you've got to scratch. Do the *thing* that came to mind as you read this, yeah that *thing* that you have put off for way too long. What are you waiting for? Do the damn *thing*.

BETTER THAN YOU COULD HAVE IMAGINED

Maybe this whole time you have been looking at it from completely the wrong perspective. Maybe things are going better than you realize. You have been so focused on what could all go wrong that you haven't noticed everything that *is going right*. What if it turns out better than you expected? What if everything falls into place and you get everything you ever wanted *and more*? What if you meet the right person at the right time? What if you end up getting that dream job, buying that dream home or going on that dream trip? What if you end up wildly successful? What if the stars aligned in *your* favor and everything worked out perfectly *for you*? This stuff happens. People end up getting more than they could have ever dreamed of. So why not you? What if *you* end up with a spectacular conclusion too? Realize that everything could *go right* for you, that things can work in *your* favor and that life is working for *you* and not *against* you. Have some faith that it could all be so much better than you could have imagined.

SO WHAT'S STOPPING YOU?

So what's stopping you? Is it your ability? No, it's not that you have proven time and time again that you are capable of *anything*. Is it your fear of failing that is stopping you? No, it can't be that either, you know failure doesn't really exist and you have always bounced back whenever you needed to. So maybe it is fear of what other people will think of you that is stopping you? No, that's not possible. You know that no one's opinion of you is worth more than your happiness and you can't miss out on what you want because someone else might not like it. *So what is stopping you then?* Where is your roadblock? If we are being honest, everything you think is stopping you right now really isn't. It is all just an excuse. It is time that you quit messing yourself around and accept that there really is *nothing stopping you* at all. You have nothing to lose. It's time to get out there and do what you want to do with your life. So let me ask you again, what's stopping you?

MAKE THIS YOUR YEAR

Make this *your* year - the year that you change it all for the better. The year that you become the person you want to be and the year that *everything* changes for you. The year you dedicate to improving, growing and bettering yourself. The year you remove anything that takes away from your happiness. Make this the year you get your finances right, your health in order and your attitude in the best place possible. Make this the year that your well-being skyrockets, the year that you raise your standards and expect better from yourself. The year that you quit making excuses, hit your goals and finally overcome your fears. Make this the year that your happiness is the priority and your inner peace non-negotiable. Decide that you are going to make this *your* year and get serious about making progress. This time next year your whole life could look completely different *or* it could look exactly the same. The choice is yours. It just takes one decision to start transforming your life and you can do that *this* year.

YOU CAN'T QUIT

Quitting is beneath you and you know it. When you are thinking of quitting you are listening to your fears instead of your strengths. Fear has gotten you nowhere, but your *strength* has carried you this far already, *so lean on that*. You have come too far to even consider quitting and if you quit now then that was all for *nothing*. Right now, you are in the middle of a hard patch, a tough spot, a challenge. But all hard patches pass, all tough spots eventually get put behind you and all challenges are there to make you grow. This is just part of the journey. Quitting is not an option so rule it out of your mind. Instead, if it feels too much right now then pause for a moment and take a breather. Rather than quit, just pause for a moment knowing that you will be continuing on your journey, but that you are allowing yourself to recharge a bit before you do. You are going to overcome this and you are going to figure this out. You are not someone who backs down when it gets tough, you rise to the occasion and finish what you started. This isn't the end, you aren't going to stop until you get where you want to go. You *will* get there. This will all be worth it and you are going to see it through, just *please* don't quit.

BE RELENTLESS

Be *relentless* in the pursuit of what you want. There is nothing stopping you and there is nothing you can't do, so let yourself chase the things that your heart and soul desire. Know that it won't always be easy. Big moves, big achievements and big victories *will* bring challenges on the way, that's just how it goes. But you need to be *relentless* the whole way. Find solutions where it looks like there aren't any, pivot and change direction as many times as it takes. Keep going and try again and again and *again* until you break through. It only takes one small crack to shatter the toughest walls, keep hammering away until you have made your way through to what you want. It is *yours* for the taking.

NON-NEGOTIABLE PROGRESS

Start making the things that matter to your life non-negotiable. Daily runs. Prayer. Meditation. 8 hours of sleep. 2 Liters of water. Time alone. Personal development. Long walks. Boundaries. Whatever it is for you, *make it matter*. Because that is how your life changes. Whatever elevates you, boosts your happiness and wellness, and brings you joy must be non-negotiable to you. You do them for yourself no matter what. It is about prioritizing your needs and burning the excuses. That is how you transform your life into a happier, healthier and more fulfilled version. Do what you need to do for your own personal progress and stop negotiating with your happiness, from now on it's a priority.

SEIZE THIS MOMENT

There is no better moment than right now. You will never feel fully ready, so if you are waiting for the perfect moment to arrive then the truth is you are going to be waiting for the rest of your life. Sometimes you just need to seize the moment right now and decide that *this* is where you start. Decide that you are not *waiting* for what you want to come to you and instead, you are going to go and *seek it out* yourself. Get started and figure it out as you go. You don't need to have all the answers right now, you just need to make the first move. Seize this moment and don't look back.

YOU CAN TRANSFORM YOUR WHOLE LIFE

Never forget that your life is *so full* of possibilities and opportunities. You are *never* stuck, rather you are incredibly free to create *anything* you want in your life at any point. You could wake up tomorrow morning and choose to make your life totally unrecognizable. You can change your body, your health, your finances. You can change where you live, you can change what you do for work. You can change your friends, fall in love, learn a new skill, learn a language or go on an adventure. You can rise from nothing to something. You can become someone new entirely. The issue is, sometimes you forget this. Sometimes you let yourself think that your current circumstances are fixed. Nothing is fixed. This life is *yours* and you get to decide what your next evolution looks like. Allow yourself to take action and let all of the extraordinary change that you want unfold in your life. Your new life is waiting for you.

ANYTHING IS POSSIBLE FOR YOU

Step into a mindset of 'anything is possible for me' and just watch how your life *unrecognizably* changes. When you let yourself believe that anything is possible your mind becomes more driven and solution-focused and as a result the course of your life changes for the better. We live in a time where anything is possible for *anyone,* and that means *you* too. There is nothing you can't do and nothing you can't be, your life is full of possibilities and opportunities and you *have* to embrace that. Picture what you want your life to be like in 1, 3 or even 5 years from now and realize that you can craft and create your life into *anything* that you can imagine. Absolutely *anything* is possible for you, you just need to let yourself believe it.

IT'S NOT OVER YET

Don't conclude too early. It's *not* over for you yet and you are *not* finished. There is more in you to go and what you see right now is *not* your final outcome. So often we make the mistake of concluding that where we are at this moment *is as good as it's going to get for us* and that we have missed our chance to get what we really want from life. Know that it's not over for you yet and that nothing is permanent. One bad job is *not* the end of your career. One bad relationship does not mean you will be alone forever. One mistake is just that - *one* mistake. A setback is just a *temporary* setback. Just because you aren't where you want to be yet doesn't mean that it is over. There is more to come for you and you can create anything you want at *any* point in your life. You can recover from anything and I mean *anything*. So don't ruin your chances of happiness by giving up on yourself too early. You've still got so many more miles in you. You are not finished and it's not over.

YOU HAVE TO OVERESTIMATE YOURSELF

What would happen if instead of constantly doubting yourself, you constantly overestimated yourself? Imagine if you lived your life thinking you could do *anything*. If you lived your life fully overestimating what you could do and believed in yourself so fiercely that nothing felt unattainable for you. It would absolutely change your life. **So do it**, start living your life with a sense of complete certainty in yourself. Why? Because *this* is how you start believing in yourself. You have to fake it until you feel it. What starts as overestimating yourself will soon turn into *real* confidence as it becomes clear that you were capable *the whole time* - you just didn't know it yet. You have to overestimate yourself and live with an unwavering and unconditional belief in yourself. Shower yourself in positive validation, *bathe* in self-confidence, and approach *everything* in your life as though you are unstoppable. Go in guns blazing, even if you need to do it absolutely terrified. You can do literally anything if you put your mind to it and *this* is how you put your mind to it, by overestimating yourself. You've got to fight your corner, even if you don't feel like it. Because it's a hard world out there and if you don't believe in yourself no one will. So go out there and overestimate yourself.

IT'S NEVER TOO LATE TO DO WHAT YOU WANT

I want to remind you that it is *never* too late for you to go after what you want in life. It is *never* too late to completely change your life in any way, shape or form and it's *never* too late to start over. It *doesn't matter* where you are starting from today, you can begin again and choose whatever path you want for yourself. The opportunity to have a great life never expires and the things you want are not time-sensitive. You can't 'miss the boat' in your own life because you are the one driving your life forward and deciding what happens next. You have *way more* time to do the things that you want to do than you think. Move country, change your career, reinvent yourself as a person, and change *every single element* of your life if that is what you want to do. So do it, make huge, crazy and unrecognizable changes in your life. It is *never* too late.

DON'T LET ANYONE TRY AND STOP YOU

Not everyone wants you to win, in fact, it will make some people more comfortable if you don't. The bigger you get, the smaller it will make some people feel. You are going to face some people who will tell you that you can't do it and others who will stand in your way. But that leaves you with two options. Option one is that you accept it, and you keep yourself small because they have scared you away from embracing your real potential. Option two is you steamroll right through that and decide that *you* are the only one who can dictate what is possible for you. Accept that you can't please everyone on your journey and that that is completely ok. It is *never* worth sacrificing your own happiness for the sake of someone else's opinion of you. Cut through all the noise and don't let anyone try to stop you. This is *your* life, you get to decide what matters.

YOU ARE LIMITLESS

Do not forget that you are *limitless*. There is nothing you cannot do and there is nothing you cannot create in your life. Anything is possible for *you*, you can be *whoever* you want to be. The issue is you have been listening to your doubts and fears for too long, you have been listening to the lie that you *can't* and ignoring the fact that you *can*. There are no rules, no limits and no reasons why you cannot have exactly what you want in life. Yes, you will have to do the work and take action, but again, that is completely within your control. If you are willing to roll up your sleeves, do your bit and get stuck in then it is absolutely possible for you. No matter what your starting point is today, you have a blank page in front of you and you get to choose exactly what the rest of your life looks like. You can turn your whole life around. You can reinvent your world. You can achieve big, huge and amazing things and you can do whatever it is that would make you happy. But it's a choice, you have to *choose* to believe that there are endless possibilities for you. You have to *choose* to make the most of your life and live exactly how you wish to.

YOU ARE THE ONLY ONE WHO CAN CHANGE YOUR LIFE

You are the only one who can make a difference in your life. No one else, only *you*. It is *you* who is going to have to be really honest about what needs to change. It is *you* who has to decide to give up those bad habits that make you feel awful and hold you back. It's *you* who has to realize that not everyone you have in your life right now actually deserves to be there, and it's *you* who has to make the change to remove them even if it's hard to do so. It is *you* who has to stand up for yourself. It is *you* who has to realize that you can do better and it is *you* who needs to take action to actually do better. It is *you* who has to be honest with yourself when a relationship isn't working, and it is *you* who has to decide to leave that toxic job. It is *you* who has to decide to take better care of your body and your mind. It is no one else's job to help you or fix things for you. This all has to come from *you*. But that's a good thing because it's also *you* who has the power to make yourself happier than you could *ever* imagine. The next move is yours to decide, you can create the most incredible life for yourself if you wish to. Because no one can stop you but *you*.

PROVE THEM ALL WRONG

You are done being underestimated, doubted and overlooked. You are done with people thinking that you haven't got it in you. *They don't really know you,* because if they did they would know not to doubt you for a second. Little do they know there is a fire in you that can *never* be put out. You are committed and focused and have a drive in you that *cannot* be stopped. You are here to prove them *all* wrong, to prove once and for all that you are *not* to be underestimated. *Do it* to see the look on their faces. *Do it* to make them realize that they never should have never overlooked you and that *you* don't back down. No one can hold you back, no one can shrink you. This is your moment to step into the spotlight. Leave them with their jaws hanging open as you claim your victory. It's time to prove them wrong and show them what you are made of.

DON'T WASTE YOUR POTENTIAL

You have so much potential. So Much. The thing is you *know* you do. Yet you let the doubt creep in and hold you back. You can't waste your potential just because you are scared or you don't feel ready enough to go after what you want. You have to remember that your potential *scares* other people, they can see what you are capable of, so make sure you can too. This is your one shot at life, *make the absolute most of it*. Your hunger is there for a *reason* and your potential is there *to be used*. Leave nothing on the table when it comes to getting what you want. Go out there and clean up. This is your moment to thrive, you owe it to yourself.

YOU GET TO DECIDE HOW THIS ENDS

Never forget the power you have over your own life. You get to decide how this ends for you, you get to decide how you shape your path and what the rest of your life looks like. *No one* else, *only you.* Cut out the noise from other people and the outside world. You run the show. So be proactive with your life, stop waiting for things to happen and instead take responsibility for *making them happen.* Take control, put the plans in motion and do the work that will give you the outcome *you* desire. You get to decide how this ends. At this point it is all unwritten, a completely blank canvas for you to go and create. It doesn't matter where you come from, what you have experienced in the past, whether you have failed, made mistakes or have regrets. That is all irrelevant, what matters is where you are going.

PEP TALKS FOR WHEN YOU NEED TO TAKE IT UP A LEVEL

IT'S YOU VERSUS YOU

At the end of the day, it's *you* versus *you*. No one else can push you forward, no one else can hold you back. You can either create things or limit things in your life. You can either work with yourself or against yourself. It will *always* be you versus you. So you have to decide what version of yourself you are going to let run your life each day. Let it be the optimist, the version who sees the best in everything. Let it be the version of you who has the discipline to do what needs to be done. Let it be the bravest version of you who is greater than your fears. Let it be the version of you that promises to get back up and try again and again. Let it be the version of you that doesn't take things personally and who nourishes your self-esteem daily. You have to make a daily conscious decision to choose the best version of you to live through. You choose your perspective and in turn, that dictates how your life will look. It will always be *you* versus *you*.

IF YOU ARE LOOKING FOR A SIGN THIS IS IT

If you are looking for a sign then, *this is it*. Please stop holding yourself back. Please stop compromising your happiness. Please make changes to your life that will give you every wonderful thing that you deserve. You deserve the absolute best and it's time that you went and got it. Do what you need to do - this is the sign you have been waiting for.

TAKE IT UP A LEVEL

What would happen if you took it up a level? Even just one level. What would happen if you stopped with the excuses, if you stopped with the procrastination and if you stopped putting things off for tomorrow? What's crazy is that you are scared of making moves that you are already *more* than capable of making. Right now your mind is your *only* barrier, but you can change that. Think about what would happen if you finally stopped holding back, if you stopped listening to your fears and insecurities and instead fully stepped into your power. You don't need to make huge leaps to make a difference, even the slightest move forward will take you closer towards your goal. So why not do it? Why not take it up *one* level? Sometimes all you need is that tiny bit of progress to make you feel like it is *actually possible*. Start chipping away at it, and slowly but surely and you will be amazed by how much that changes your course. No more wasting your own time and delaying your own progress - you are ready for this next move.

RAISE YOUR STANDARDS

Your life will only be as good as the standards you hold yourself to. The difference between where you are *now* and where you *want* to be is the standards that you set yourself. You can transform your whole life - your relationships, friendships, your finances, your home, your fitness level, *anything* - by raising your standards. Your whole world will change dramatically if you are prepared to raise your standards to match what you *actually* want to see for yourself. Be honest with yourself about where your standards are not high enough. Where can you do better for yourself? Put the bar higher and watch your whole life transform. You can do this, raise your standards.

WHAT WOULD THE BEST VERSION OF YOU DO

What would the best version of you be doing right now? How would they spend their day? What time do they get up? What do they eat? How do they prioritize their health? Do they work out? Who do they spend time with? What are they working on? What are their goals? What do they care about? Whose opinions do they prioritize? How do they feel about themselves? What are their non-negotiables? What are the standards they live by? What do they read? We all make the mistake of thinking it's so hard to know what to do to get where we want to get, but actually it's a lot more obvious than we think. Think about the best version of you, the version of you who is living *exactly* as you would love to be living. The version of you who doesn't let fear hold them back. The version of you that doesn't care what other people think. The version of you who is willing to play full out and see what they are truly capable of. That is your answer right there. Do what that version of you would be doing, adopt their lifestyle and tweak your current behaviors to match theirs. Make small changes each day to be more like the person you want to be and bit by bit slowly your life is going to evolve.

YOU ARE READY

You have been waiting until you feel ready, but what you need to understand is that you are ready now. You don't need to plan anymore, you don't need to wait for anything else. You're ready as you are right now and there's nothing else you need to do before you take the leap. *So take the leap.* You can't keep wasting your own time because your fear is telling you that you aren't ready. **You are.** So go for it and figure it out as you go.

BET ON YOURSELF

Everything changes when you decide to get out of your own way and finally bet on yourself. If there is one person on this earth that you should be willing to go all in on, it is *you*. Bet on *yourself*. The truth is if you are not betting *on* yourself, you are betting *against* yourself and you cannot live your life holding yourself back like that. You bet on yourself by saying **'yes'** to opportunities *even* if you don't feel ready. You bet on yourself when you step out of your comfort zone and *trust* yourself to figure it out. You bet on yourself when you take action and ask for what you want. You bet on yourself when you stop making excuses and decide to give it *everything* you've got. You bet on yourself when you stop waiting for the perfect circumstances and instead start where you are. You are going to be blown away by how much you will accomplish when you *finally* bet on yourself and take action to bring it to life. People less capable than you succeed at the things you want, simply because they are willing to *bet on themselves*. You are the safest bet you could ever make, it is yours for the taking.

DECIDE

Decide to do better. Decide to be braver. Decide to start over. Decide to push your limits. Decide to prioritize yourself. Decide to take the leap. Decide to find out who you really are. Decide you are ready. Decide to commit. Decide to take it up a level. Decide to only accept the best for yourself. Decide to forgive. Decide to take better care of your heart, your body, your mind and your soul. Decide to pursue happiness over everything. Decide to make your life completely different starting today.

BECOME BULLETPROOF

Bulletproof. You have to become *bulletproof.* Your self-esteem and your confidence are *yours* and yours alone and nothing outside of you can harm them. No matter what is said or done to you, you can never let it affect you or bring you down. You are *above that.* If you let every little bit of nonsense someone says or thinks about you seep into your view of who you are, you are going to lose your way pretty quickly. **Protect yourself.** Let whatever is thrown at you ricochet off of you and have no effect on you at all. Your self-worth needs to be untouchable, never wavering and never questioned. Regardless of what the outside world thinks, says or does to you, you must stand firmly in the opinion that you *are* and *always will be* enough. Life is tough and to survive it you need thick skin. Don't take anything personally, you know who you are, you know what you are capable of and no one's opinion of you can take that away from you. Nothing can put a dent in your armor, **you are bulletproof.**

NO MORE EXCUSES

No more excuses. No more telling yourself you can't when you can. No more doubting yourself and making up reasons why you can't go and get what you want from your life. Remember, you are the one running the show. You set the tone of your life with what you let yourself believe. Anything is possible if you would only just give yourself a chance. Quit the excuses, change the narrative and get out of your own way.

RISE TO THE OCCASION

Life is going to kick you around a little bit. It's nothing personal, it happens to everyone. It will push you and test you and when that happens you need to rise to the occasion. You can't take life's challenges lying down. Give as good as you get, because *you* don't give up that easily. Other people might, but not *you*. Keep going until you get what you want. Remember that you have walked through walls to get to where you are now. You shouldn't have made it this far, *but you did*. Drag that fighting spirit out and remind yourself that nothing can defeat you. You can't let yourself be discouraged *easily* because life isn't going to go *easy* on any of us. No matter how exhausted and defeated you feel, recognize that you are still standing and that is *all* that matters. You are still here and you are going to keep going until it gets better. Pride will recover, bruised egos heal, and that fire within you will *always* rage on. So *rise* to the occasion and don't let anything stop you.

DON'T WAIT

Don't wait. Life is too short; don't wait to do what you want to do. Just do it. Take action, take the plunge, take everything life has to offer. You have no good *reason* to wait, rather what you have is a bunch of *excuses* that make you think you should wait. But those excuses won't take you to where you want to go or make you who you want to be. Whatever you think you are waiting for is not going to make a spot of difference. Make the moves you want to make *now* and in doing so give yourself the adventure of a lifetime.

REMEMBER WHERE YOU STARTED

I know that you have further to go and that you aren't where you want to be yet, but please remember where you started. You started on the back foot and yet you have still managed to build yourself up to an enviable height. Yes, you may be neck and neck with others from an outside perspective but don't forget that you started in different places. You have had to come *so much further* to get here. Whilst they took the elevator, you took the stairs and had to painstakingly climb your way to the same spot. *That matters.* You had to work so much harder to get yourself here. What was handed to them *you* had to earn. You have earned your spot at the top, through determination, grit and unmatched drive. Yes, sometimes you may feel behind those around you, but you need to remember that you built and shaped your life with your bare hands and without any help. Realize how far you have come and how impressive that really is.

LIFE IS ABOUT UPGRADES, NOT DOWNGRADES

Be honest with yourself, is what you are doing right now an upgrade to your life or a downgrade? It's going to be one or the other. Every action, thought, decision and activity is going to be either an upgrade or downgrade to your life. There is no other option and even the small things matter. Those incremental small daily upgrades to your life eventually add up to the most incredible transformations. Just like those small incremental downgrades slowly and gradually bring you down to less than you deserve. Life is *always* about making upgrades and not downgrades. In everything you do, choose the best for yourself. Take the upgrade even if it's the harder route because it will always pay off in the long run. That is the mistake so many people make, they unknowingly take the downgrade because it's easier. Downgrades don't always look like downgrades, they look like compromises, shortcuts and excuses that you tell yourself. *This all matters.* Stay focused on improving the quality of your life every single day in everything you do. Upgrades aren't always the easiest option, but you don't want easy, *you want better.*

THERE IS NO NEXT TIME

How many times have you put off what you wanted for 'next time'? How many times have you promised yourself that next time you will go for it? Next time you will be braver. Next time you will say what you need to say. Next time you will shoot your shot. Next time you will take the opportunity. Next time, next time, next time. We forget that *this is it*. This is our one chance at this lifetime. There is no next time. You need to make this matter *now*. You need to make this count *now*. You really don't have anything to lose so you may as well go out there full force and push for what you want *this time*. Make moves, take risks and do the things that you don't feel brave enough to do. Because there is no next time.

ASK FOR WHAT YOU WANT

You have to be brave enough to ask for what you want. You can't expect to get what you want if you aren't brave enough to put yourself out there and make your requests known. Imagine not being considered for an opportunity just because no one knew you wanted it. Be forward. Put yourself on the radar of the things you want. Make it clear where you are trying to get to. Let yourself be the person who comes to mind for opportunities because you made people aware of your goals. If you don't ask, you don't get. What is the worst that could happen if you ask for what you want? You get a no. At least you know you tried. But equally, what if you get a *yes*? *Yes* to exactly what you want. So shoot your shot constantly, and make it clear what your game plan is. Sometimes in order to have doors open for you, you have to be prepared to *shove* the door open yourself and not be scared of any resistance. Ask for what you want. Other people go out there and ask for what *they* want and do you know what? Quite often they get it.

100-YEAR-OLD YOU

One day if you are lucky you are going to be gray and old, and at that point, you are going to look back at your life and realize that you had nothing to lose the whole time. 100-year-old you is going to look back and wonder why on earth you spent so much time worrying? Why did you care so much about what you weighed or how you looked? 100-year-old you is going to wonder why you didn't pursue your dreams and take risks? The whole time you had nothing to lose and everything to gain. 100-year-old you is going to wonder why you didn't travel and treat your life like an adventure? 100-year-old you isn't going to care what people thought of you or their opinions of your life. It's your life and you only get to do this once, *so do it*. **Live.** Really live. When you come face to face with 100-year-old you, you want to be so damn proud of how you lived. You want to know that you lived fully and happily and did not give a damn about the small things that really don't matter.

LIFE GIVES YOU WHAT YOU ASK FOR

Life will always give you what you ask for, so make sure that you are asking for the *very best* for yourself. You set the tone and choose the direction of your life based on what you think is possible for you. Your expectations for yourself shape the way your life ends up looking. So expect the *very best* for yourself. Because you're going to get exactly what you *allow* yourself to believe you are deserving of. So set those expectations as high as you can. Life gives you what you ask for, *so ask for it*. Put yourself out there and make it clear what you want. Chase after opportunities, bet on yourself and start saying yes to what excites you - even if you don't feel ready. Nothing is *too* big, *too* good or *too* much for you. Life is rooting for you and so you need to root for yourself too and that starts with being brave enough to *actually* go after what you want.

TREAT YOUR LIFE LIKE AN ADVENTURE

Start seeing your life as an adventure, *because it is*. You don't need to take everything so seriously as if one wrong move will have it all come crashing down. It won't. Life is far more robust than that. You can explore, play, experiment and treat your life like an adventure because your time on this earth is meant to be enjoyed. So don't hold back. Do the things that your soul craves, the things that light you up inside and make you feel alive. You have this one big, bold, beautiful life to live, so go out there and *actually live*. Do the things that *scare* you, do the things that *excite* you and explore all the possibilities that are out there for you. Think of all the things that could go *right*, and embrace all of the opportunities that lay ahead of you. There is nothing you need to fear in this life, it is just one big adventure.

WHAT DO YOU WANT?

What do you want? No really, what is it that you want for your life? Most people cannot answer the simple question, 'What do you want?' and yet despite not knowing what they want, they are somehow convinced they are going to get it. Don't fumble your way through your life. You need to know where you are going. You need to know what the vision for your life is - *you need to know what you want*. You have an incredible opportunity in front of you to carve out and design your life. *So do it*. It's time you figured out what you actually want.

SOMETIMES YOU JUST NEED A PEP TALK

PEP TALKS TO REASSURE YOU

JUST A LITTLE REMINDER

This is just a little reminder that: It *is* ok to make mistakes and get it wrong. That getting your heartbroken broken *won't* hurt forever. That rejection *isn't* personal. That you are making more progress than you realize. That you *are* on a good path. That life is short so don't sweat the small stuff. That you are loved. That good things happen to *you*. That you have overcome every challenge you have faced so far. That you haven't met everyone you are going to meet yet. That it all works out in the end. That no one is judging you as much as you think. That where you are now isn't where you will always be. That if you have to force it, it probably isn't right for you. That great things are coming your way. That you are better looking than you think you are. That your future is bright. That you are worthy and enough as you are. That you have *nothing* to fear. That all you have is this moment so enjoy it. That you deserve the best. That no one gets to dictate your worth but you.

YOUR LIFE IS NOT SUPPOSED TO BE PERFECT

Understand that your life is *not* supposed to be perfect. No one is perfect, no one has a perfect life and absolutely *no one* expects you to be perfect. So please don't expect yourself to be perfect either. Life is imperfect and that imperfection is *liberating*. Stop being so hard on yourself and free yourself from the pressure of trying to live immaculately, it is *not* realistic or necessary. Know that despite your life not being perfect it is still a massive success. You are human, and therefore you are supposed to have flaws and those flaws make your life *more* exciting. Give yourself a break, you are doing great.

SOMETIMES LIFE LOOKS MESSIER THAN IT IS

It's important that you realize that you can be *exactly* where you need to be in life but life can still feel hard and look messy. Be reassured that it *looks* messier than it actually is, because often when it all feels like it is falling apart it is actually all coming together as it should be. It's just hard to see that from where you are right now. Take a step back and look at the bigger picture of where you are. This process of evolution was never going to feel smooth and easy, real transformation involves lots of moving parts and you are going to need to uproot yourself a little. Don't confuse the magic of what is happening with something negative, this is an incredible period of growth and transformation for you. It is like a puzzle when you first tip it out of the box, there are pieces thrown everywhere making it impossible to see the finished picture. Until one day all of the pieces slot into place and *finally* make sense in a way that is so much better than you could ever have imagined. Don't confuse the process of progress with a mess, this is not a mess, this is a masterpiece in the making.

YOU ARE NOT BEHIND

Give yourself a break. Life is not a race and you are not behind. There is no rush, there is no competition and there is *nowhere* in particular that you should be right now. Go at your own pace. There is no such thing as being behind in life, just like there is no such thing as being ahead. We are each on our own journey and no two journeys will ever be the same. They are not comparable, nor should we want to compare them. It doesn't matter to your life what other people are doing with theirs. It is not you versus them, it's *you* versus *you*. You are a better version of yourself than you were previously, that is what matters. It is impossible to fall behind on your own journey, it's *your* journey and it happens on its own time in its own way. If you are not where you want to be right now then please remember that your story isn't over. There is so much more to come for you and it is all happening exactly when it is meant to.

ZOOM OUT

Sometimes you need to zoom out of your own life and look at it from a distance. Because when you do that you will realize that things aren't actually as bad as they seem and that it's all going better than you have let yourself believe. Things just look so much more intense and worse than they actually are when you are zoomed right in and analyzing every minute detail of your life. If you would just take a step back, you would realize that things are actually ok, pretty good in fact and that you have *a lot* to be proud of and grateful for. Give yourself the credit you deserve, you are amazing and if you would just zoom out and see it from someone else's perspective, I think you would see that too.

YOU CAN START OVER WHENEVER YOU WANT

You are always *just beginning* and you can choose to start over whenever you want. It is never too late. You can reinvent yourself and make your life look completely different starting *today*. Life isn't a straight line or one direction only kind of thing - *even though we are all guilty of expecting it to be at points*. So as we navigate through life we will all take paths that end up being the wrong ones for us, *and that is ok*. Where you are now, or who you have been in the past is not a fixed definition of you. You can change, evolve, grow and adapt in any way you see fit. Nothing is permanent, you can hit refresh and start again. You get to decide what is next for you and every day is an opportunity to start fresh. Open yourself up to the possibility that things *can* change for you, nothing is set in stone.

YOU ARE STRONGER THAN YOU THINK

You have overcome every challenge that you have had to face so far. You have rebuilt yourself back up from even your darkest of days. You have never been defeated, never shied away and never quit *even* when you wanted to. You have shown strength, courage, resilience and tenacity and it all came from *you*. Only *you*. Which proves one thing - you have *nothing* to fear. You are so much stronger than you think you are. Give yourself some credit and hold your head high, step out into the world and fear *nothing*. Because nothing can defeat you, just like nothing has ever come close to defeating you before now. Everything you have been through has built you into something incredible. So don't you dare ever doubt yourself or question your ability. You have proven what you are made of. You have proven that you can handle anything. You are not to be underestimated - *not even by yourself.* Because there is nothing you cannot do.

REJECTION DOESN'T DEFINE YOU

Rejection doesn't define you, it is something you will recover from, grow from and eventually you will heal from. A big part of changing how you feel about rejection is realizing that it isn't personal. *This isn't about you.* So many factors go into why you are being rejected and none of them mean that you aren't enough. Rejection is actually something to be proud of. It means you're going for something, you can't be rejected if you're not pushing and trying for something, whether it be a job, person, business, or relationship. So first of all, congratulations on stepping up, being bold and putting yourself out there. Not everyone does this. Know it's not over, you can still have what you want, you just need to readjust the route you take. The rest of your life is unwritten. You get to decide where you go from here, what you do and how far you reach and no rejection will ever change that.

SOMETIMES THINGS HAVE TO HAPPEN FIRST

Life doesn't always make sense, why haven't you gotten what you wanted by now? Why hasn't it all fallen into place yet? *Relax.* What you want is on its way to you but sometimes things have to happen first. Everything has its time and place. You still have things to learn, people to meet and places to see. You still have thrilling moments that you need to experience first and all of this is going to prepare you for getting what you want. It's like the warm-up before the main event. Nothing is a coincidence, if you are being made to wait for what you want there is a good reason. Something big is coming for you. Whilst you were making plans for yourself, life was busy making *even better* ones. How many times have you seen this happen, you think you have it all figured out and then *boom* life hits you with something even better. You can't rush these things, instead, you need to surrender to life's timings. Hindsight is a powerful thing and one day you will look back and realize that it all worked out perfectly, life has your back far more than you realize.

YOU CAN'T MESS UP

It is so easy to get into that cycle of worry that if you *dare* give it a shot you could mess up and ruin everything. The thing is, life really doesn't work like that. Everything is fixable, there is always a way to get back up, to turn a negative into a positive and get to where you want to go. The risk of messing it up isn't what is going to ruin your chances of success, the real threat is when you are *too fearful* to even give it a go. Fear stops you from taking the action you need to - that's the real killer of dreams. The worst thing you could do right now is *not* try, that is the only way you can truly mess up. Everything else is a lesson, a learning curve, a moment of growth for you. You *have* to try, you have to give it a go and see what you can do. Discover what amazing heights you can reach and the adventures you can have. If you don't try you will spend the rest of your life wondering what *could have been*. There is nothing to lose, back yourself and do it.

GOOD THINGS HAPPEN TO YOU

Good things happen *to* you and good things happen *for* you. I know you have had more than your fair share of challenges and at times it felt like nothing was going right for you. But the chapter has changed and now in this chapter, it's *your* turn to thrive. It's your turn to be happy, your turn to win and your turn to receive blessing after blessing after blessing. From now on good things happen for *you*, opportunities are going to come your way and you are going to experience the most amazing moments. Good things happen to you and you are *so* deserving of them.

REJECTION IS REDIRECTION

Even if you don't understand it at the time, rejection is always redirection for something better. Be grateful for all of the closed doors, the no's and the disappointments, those moments were working in your favor and leading you to something better. Every time you got rejected from what you wanted it happened for a reason. Whatever is meant for you will always be yours and will always find you. Know that rejection is working *for you*, there is a better path, a better outcome, a better place for you to end up and the rejection you face is simply making sure you don't settle for less than that. Eventually, you will get there, the penny will drop and you will get what you wanted all along. You will then realize that the rejection was just gentle nudges leading you in the right direction.

LOOK HOW FAR YOU HAVE COME

Do you remember the days when you didn't even know what you wanted? You were so unsure of what move to make next and so worried about how it would all come together. *But look at you now.* You know who you are now. You know what you want and you know what you don't. You have grown so much as a person and you have conquered so many things that you never thought you could. It is breathtaking to look at you and see all that you have overcome and how much you have achieved. Although you may not have hit every one of your goals yet, you have still done incredible things with your life. Know that you don't need to be perfect in order to be proud of yourself. You have overcome so much, you have learnt from your mistakes, you have dusted yourself off and let nothing defeat you. Your life is magnificent.

EVERYTHING WILL BE OK IN THE END

Although this current chapter of your life may not make sense right now, remember that this is *just a chapter*. Every chapter has to come to an end, this moment will pass and will one day be a distant memory. So if this chapter is particularly hard for you, then be assured that nothing lasts forever, *not even this*. One day you will wake up and find that you are in a new chapter, a better chapter and that you survived everything that you are facing. Everything will be ok in the end.

IT'S NOT AS BIG OF A DEAL AS YOU THINK

I know this feels huge in your life right now, but I promise you it really isn't as big of a deal as you think. You are overthinking the situation because it feels so significant, but that is giving it more power over you than it deserves. Whatever you are facing right now is really not as big of a deal as you are imagining, it won't matter in the future, and it barely matters now. It just feels big in your mind and it feels bigger for you than everyone else because it involves you. Trust me, no one cares about this as much as you do. So please, don't give yourself a hard time over this. Forget this and let it go. *It really is ok*. Everyone is going to move on from this. Time is going to work in your favor and as the weeks, months and years go past the relevance of this will vanish. You can't lose sleep over this, it's not as big of a deal as you think.

GIVE IT TIME

Whether you like it or not, things take time. Deep down you know this, yet you still give yourself a hard time if you don't accomplish everything you want overnight. It was *never* going to happen overnight, so please don't be so hard on yourself because it hasn't happened yet. Great things take time and just because you aren't where you want to be yet doesn't mean you won't get there. You will, but it's going to take trial and error. It's going to involve mistakes, revised plans and starting over. Be kind to yourself, you are doing the best you can and you *will* get there. Things always take longer than we initially imagine so don't panic if progress is slower than you expected. One day it will all fall into place and when that day comes you will be able to see with complete clarity and certainty that it *had* to take as long as it did. Focus on doing your part. Show up, play your role, put the effort in, forget how long it is taking and above all *trust* that it's all going to be ok.

DON'T WORRY ABOUT THE FUTURE

Just a little reminder that every single thing is falling into place for you, perfectly. Just as it is meant to. Instead of *worrying* about the future, get *excited* about it. The universe doesn't make mistakes, it's not going to leave you hanging. It has a plan for you. Everything you want and need has been taken into consideration and it is all going to work out. Your life *today* may not look how you want it to, but you aren't finished yet. One day you'll look back in amazement as you realize that the whole time everything was aligning for you. So for now, do your bit to move your life forward and then *trust* that it is all under control. You don't have to worry about the future, the future is taking care of itself. You are perfectly on track so let it all unfold for you, it's going to be even better than you imagined.

ONE DAY IT WILL ALL MAKE SENSE

Maybe you are reading this at a point in your life where you can't believe that what is happening in your life is actually happening, or that where you are right now is really where you are. I know this is all a lot right now, but I promise you that one day you will look back and it will all make sense. Maybe this experience had to happen in order to grow you, maybe it needed to happen to show you a better path. Whatever chaos there is right now *is* leading you to where you need to be. There is *never* a struggle without a reward to follow. Every challenge you face will lead you to something better, that's just how it works. Once you have experienced everything you needed to experience, learnt everything that you need to learn and grown where you needed to grow you will look back and finally understand why it needed to happen. This was all part of the journey and it is shaping you for the better in some way.

ALL ROADS LEAD TO THE RIGHT DESTINATION

Don't worry, you aren't going to mess this up. You are going to get to exactly where you want to be. You are going to do everything you want to do, and you are going to find what makes you happy. So please stop worrying about making mistakes or taking wrong turns. You cannot take a wrong path in life, every path you take is a necessary part of your journey and all roads *will* lead you to the right destination. Life isn't as fragile as you think, you can't ruin it all by taking a few wrong turns. You will *always* be led back to where you belong. *Have more faith.* Life is an adventure, it's meant to be enjoyed. You are meant to explore, experiment and take chances. So do exactly that and know that you will always land on your feet. There are so many amazing moments that lay ahead of you, don't waste them by worrying about getting it wrong. All roads will lead you to where you need to be, so enjoy the journey.

NO ONE KNOWS WHAT THEY ARE DOING

Don't worry if you don't have it all figured out by now. Nobody does. Each and every one of us is simply winging our way through life and trying to make the most of it as we go. Which is why it's *absolutely ok* if you don't have it all figured out either. The truth is you don't need to have it all figured out in order to be ok. You are going to be ok regardless. Not only is it impossible to have it all figured out because life is so wildly unpredictable, but half of the fun is figuring it out as you go. Have fun with it. Let yourself make mistakes. Let yourself explore and experiment and if things go wrong simply get up and try again. So if you, *like the rest of us*, don't know what you are doing then *congratulations*, welcome to the club and make yourself at home.

YOU ARE SO CLOSE

I know you have had to wait patiently and I know that it feels so far away, but I promise you are so much closer than you think. Your hard work is paying off, your patience is being rewarded and your time is coming. It will all be so worth it in the end, it will all make sense and the timing will feel so perfect for you. You are so close to getting what you want. Your moment is approaching and it is all going to fall into place so spectacularly. Hold on in there, you are on the final lap, keep pushing.

NEW DOORS ARE ALWAYS OPENING

Don't panic if you aren't where you want to be right now. You never know what is waiting for you just around the corner. New doors are constantly opening for you and new opportunities are always making their way onto your path. Your role in this is simply to be *open* to these new adventures and to always be *willing* to expand yourself and try something new. You never know what is coming next, there are so many amazing things that life has planned for you. Have faith in the fact that you are going to end up exactly where you want to be and most of all let yourself *enjoy* the process of getting there.

YOU ARE OK

Maybe it's not as bad as you think, maybe you're just spiraling and letting things feel bigger than they are right now. Maybe you are doubting yourself at this moment and instead, you need to remember who you are and what you are capable of. *You are ok,* things are ok and it is *all* going fine. Let yourself relax in this moment and know that you are ok and that your life is in a great place.

I KNOW HOW IT ENDS FOR YOU

I know it feels overwhelming right now, but rest assured I know how it ends for you. It ends with everything falling into place. All the things that you are working so hard for, all of your hopes and dreams and wishes coming together, even better than you imagined. It ends with you realizing that all the hard work and struggles were worth it, everything that you gave came back to you tenfold. It ends with you understanding that every challenge was a lesson and a blessing that brought you to where you needed to be. It ends with you knowing that everything had to happen just how it did, that every curve ball, every close door, every rejection was actually life correcting your course leading you to something better. It ends with you realizing that dreams really do come true and you are finally living yours. This is what is waiting for you if you *just keep going.* No matter how hard it is right now, you absolutely can't quit because I know how it ends and it ends so well for you.

THERE IS ENOUGH ABUNDANCE TO GO AROUND

Somewhere along the line we seem to have bought into the belief that there is a limited amount of abundance to be had. A limited amount of success, money, opportunities, romantic partners and even happiness. Therefore if someone else is getting what we want, we panic and think that means *we can't have it too* - as if we have missed out because the other person has claimed the last bit of abundance. The truth is there is enough for anyone and everyone who wants it, but to tap into it your focus needs to be on *you*. Focus on getting yourself to where you need to be and know that you can have everything you want. There isn't only one winner. We can all win, there is an abundance to go around and that includes *for you*.

IT WILL BE WORTH IT IN THE END

Let me reassure you that it will all be worth it in the end. That eventually you will get to where you want to and you will look back and see that every single moment of this was worth it. Every bit of frustration, every time you wanted to quit - *but thankfully didn't* - was all worth it in the end. You will look back and see that you were making more progress at the time than you realized. You can't imagine this right now because you are still in the thick of it but be assured that there are victories unfolding for you at this very moment and things are falling into place. You are well on your way to where you want to be. Stay focused and keep your eyes glued on the end goal. Anyone who has ever achieved something incredible has been where you are right now. They too wondered if their effort would ever pay off, wondered why it was so tough and hoped and prayed that it would be worth it in the end. And it was, just like it will be worth it in the end for you. You are closer than you think.

YOU CAN HANDLE MORE THAN YOU THINK

You worry about the future, the past and everything in between. You worry about change, challenges and messing up. But you are forgetting one key thing, no matter what comes your way, you *can* handle it. You can handle way more than you think you can. You are forgetting just how resilient you are and just how capable you are of navigating your way through whatever life throws you. There is nothing you won't survive, nothing you won't be able to tackle and nothing you can't handle. No matter what comes your way you *will* find a way to make it work and you *will* be ok. In fact, better than ok. Because nothing can ever tear you down to a point that you can't recover from. You will *always* get back up. You overestimate how big a challenge is and underestimate how well you will overcome it. You forget how incredibly strong you are. You have proven that you can count on yourself to figure it out like you always have. You have been facing and conquering challenges your whole life and you're still here to tell the tale. You adapt, you are resilient, you tackle it and you win. You always bounce back and next time will be no different. Truthfully, you can handle far more than you think.

IT WILL HAPPEN

I know you want amazing things for yourself, and so you should, but you also need some patience to go with it. It *will* happen, but in its own time. You are quick to give yourself timeframes and deadlines for when you want things to happen, but honestly, were those time frames ever realistic? Often the time frames we set for ourselves are impossible from the get-go and yet we hold ourselves to them regardless and feel bad about ourselves when we don't hit them. I want to remind you that *it is going to happen,* you are going to get what you want and it's all going to fall into place for you. However, you need to accept that some things take time and it might not be to your schedule. There is no rush, just take your time. What you are chasing *will* be yours, just keep your head down and keep working on it and it will slot all into place. Life works to perfect timing and if you knew what was on its way to you, you wouldn't mind waiting for it just a little longer.

PEOPLE LIKE YOU WAY MORE THAN YOU THINK

You are so much more liked than you realize. That voice in your head that doubts how likable you are is wrong. It's fueled by anxiety, self-doubt and fear and *cannot* be trusted. We always overestimate how much we are disliked and underestimate how much we are liked and valued by others. Sometimes you are blind and cannot see how valued you really are. You are *so* wanted and you *matter* to people. People are excited to see you and feel blessed to be part of your life. You have so many great qualities about you, but *you* need to let yourself really believe this. You can't keep hurting yourself by listening to the parts of you that are wounded. The parts of you which are too scared to believe how much you can be wanted. People are drawn to you, they want to know you and spend time with you. Some even want to be like *you*. You may not realize it but there would be a big hole in their lives if you weren't in it. You don't need to change a single thing about you to be liked. You are so valued and wanted *just as you are.*

BE PATIENT

Be patient. Just because you are not where you want to be right now doesn't mean you won't get there eventually. That is just your fear talking. When what we want isn't happening, we panic that this is it for us, that this is as good as it gets and the issue with that is truthfully we want more for ourselves then what we have currently. Where you are right now is not permanent, you are closer to what you want then you think. Everything can change for you in a heartbeat and when it does you will wonder why you ever worried so much. Things are happening in the background, and everything is coming together. It is all going to work out as you need it to. Be patient with yourself.

IT GETS EASIER AND IT IS WORTH IT

I want to remind you that it gets easier and it is worth it. Know that every step you take in the right direction will pay off tenfold. It won't be this hard forever. Doing what is best for you is not always easy, sometimes you need to do what is difficult just because it is what's best. No hardship lasts forever, no challenge is permanent, it will get easier with *every* step that you take. You grow more when times are challenging then when they are good. When you look at your life a year from now and you see the person you have become, you will see how it was worth it was and how much that growth needed to happen. You will see that even if it was tough, things did eventually fall into place and you got the biggest reward for staying the course. It gets *easier* and it *is* worth it.

PROGRESS DOSEN'T ALWAYS LOOK LIKE PROGRESS

Sometimes it might look like you are not moving forward or making the progress that you desperately want to make, but please don't let this fool you. Progress doesn't always look like progress. When you hit challenges, hurdles and blockers along your journey you are not going to feel like you are making the progress that you want. But this is *all* part of the process. What can look like chaos, is actually positive change. What looks like a hurdle, can be the springboard you need to get you to where you want to go. One day you will realize that the whole time you were making monumental progress, you just couldn't see it when you were in the thick of the action. The challenge is to not give up, not doubt yourself and not let your emotions get the better of yourself during this time. You are making far more progress than you think.

EVERY DAY IS A BLANK CANVAS

If you feel like you've messed up, or are stuck in a rut and you aren't where you want to be then please know that every day is a blank canvas for you to start again. Today is day *one* and you can leave it all behind you, start again and take your life in any direction you want to. It might not happen overnight, but it *can* change that is what matters. Regardless of where you are now and what your life looks like currently, tomorrow will always provide a blank canvas of opportunity.

YOU ARE DOING BETTER THAN YOU THINK

You are doing way better than you think you are. You put far too much pressure on yourself to be doing more and making bigger moves, because you haven't let yourself realize that you are *already* making big moves. Don't be so hard on yourself. When all you do is focus on what you have left to do you miss out on enjoying the results of what you have already done. You are reaching new highs every day and you are always moving forward *and that is what matters.* So relax, your path is already great and you deserve to feel good about yourself *right now*. You are doing better than you think, you are more capable than you think, more accomplished and more worthy than you are letting yourself realize. You are on a great path and you deserve to be proud of yourself. Remember that where you are now is only part way through the journey. You are doing so much better than you think.

YOUR TIME WILL COME

It can be so hard when it seems like everyone around you is winning, getting what they want and watching their lives fall into place, all the while you are sitting and watching and waiting patiently for your turn. But please know that your time will come too. There will be a point when it's *your turn* to have the big wins, when you are getting what *you* want, and when you cannot believe how marvelously your life's falling into place. The wait is hard, but the wait won't matter when your time comes and you get to experience everything that you have waited so patiently for. Life is incredibly fair, it won't let you down, you will get your fair share of the joy too. So be grateful for what you have now and be full of hope and excitement for what is to come. Because your time will come.

PROGRESS

Maybe the focus right now *isn't* reaching the end goal, maybe the focus is just being one step closer than you were yesterday. Sometimes what you really need to do is just focus on the progress, make any form of progress that you can. Even if it's the tiniest step in the right direction *you are still moving forward.* The small steps add up over time, do enough of those small steps and you will see a real change. Sometimes there's so much noise and so many things that we think we should be doing, when really, we just need to strip it down and decide what one thing will make the most impact right now and do that. Focus on *that*.

ONE DAY YOU WILL BE GRATEFUL THAT YOU DIDN'T GET WHAT YOU WANTED

I know it feels like you have missed out this time but trust me you have lost nothing. If you didn't get what you wanted it is *always* because life has something better planned for you. Right now it hurts, but one day you will be *grateful* that it happened like this. Each closed door and missed opportunity was life redirecting you to something *better*. Each letdown and disappointment was preparing you for something bigger. Rather than seeing this as a failure, see it as a course correction. Maybe you were heading in the wrong direction and so life has to take you off of that path and put you on a better one. One day you will know why you went through this, and you will realize that when it felt like it was all falling apart it was actually all coming together. You just couldn't see it at the time. You can't even begin to imagine all the incredible things that life has planned for you, you have no idea what is waiting just around the corner from this situation.

PEP TALKS TO BOOST YOUR SELF-ESTEEM

TALK TO YOURSELF

Talk to yourself *constantly*. Tell yourself how amazing you are. Congratulate yourself. Bathe yourself in praise. Smother yourself with words of encouragement. Don't let a single bad word about yourself slip through the net. Keep it positive and uplifting, *always.* Remind yourself daily that you belong, that you are worthy and that you matter. That you are spectacular and that there is nothing you can't do. Be obsessed with yourself and in return *watch* how your confidence grows. You have to be your own biggest supporter. *You* are your forever person. For the rest of your life you are your only constant. Therefore, you have to treat yourself right. You need to nourish your soul and become your biggest admirer. You have to care for *yourself* better than anyone could ever care for you. You are going to believe whatever you tell yourself, so make sure you are saying something nice.

HAVE MAIN CHARACTER ENERGY IN YOUR LIFE

Remember that *you* are the main character in your life. Not the sidekick, not the extra, not a spectator. The *main* character. You can't watch your life from the sidelines, your place is right in the center of the action. *You* are the main event. This whole production is about *you*. So start living like it, be *significant* in your own life. Main character energy is making yourself a priority, prioritizing your wants and needs and recognizing your own worth. It is about being confident and comfortable in who you are and proudly embracing every single part yourself, including each flaw and imperfection. It is no longer needing the approval of others or needing others to tell you that you are good enough. Because you already absolutely know you are good enough - *you are the main character after all*. It's about treating yourself right and *only* letting people spend time with you if they treat you right too. Construct your life with a narrative that works for *you*, start living on your own terms instead of living for others. It's time you start believing in yourself right to the very core of your being, even when no one else does. You are the main character, it's time you start acting like it.

YOUR YOUNGER SELF WOULD BE SO PROUD OF YOU RIGHT NOW

There is a younger version of you who would give *anything* to be where you are right now. Think about it, so much of what you used to wish for is actually your reality right now. It is incredible to see who you have become. You are living proof that you can do anything that you put your mind to, and your younger self would be *so* proud of you. You did it, *you really did it*. You overcame everything you were scared of, and you defeated everything that you thought would stop you. You beat the odds and got back up every single time. You exceeded your wildest expectations of yourself. Understand that none of that was given to you, it was you who made it happen, it was you who walked through the challenges and came out the other side as the person you are today. You may still have things that you want to do and goals you've yet to reach but it is important that you appreciate how far you've come already. Never say 'I can't' again, you have proven to that younger version of you time and time again that you *absolutely can.*

YOU ARE NOT SUPPOSED TO BE PERFECT

You are supposed to be flawed, you are supposed to be different and there is no one ideal or one perfect way to be. Life is messy, for everyone, not just you. But it is that same mess that makes life beautiful and meaningful. You don't need to fix everything in your life in order to be happy. Real happiness comes when you start to see the value, magic and blessings in your imperfect life, with its challenges, problems and flaws. *You are not supposed to be perfect.* No one got dealt the perfect hand in life. No one. We all have our things that keep us up at night or that we have to work through. No one is exempt and so instead of being envious of what you perceive to be 'perfect' in other peoples lives, make the most of what you have in yours. Your life is wonderful.

TAKE UP SPACE

Let yourself take up space. Remember that you are not here to be silenced or overlooked. Your voice matters too, just as much as anyone else's. Speak up, let yourself be heard and don't feel guilty about it. Let people know *who you are* and *what you stand for*. Make your needs known and your opinions heard. Take up the space that is rightfully yours and no longer let others steamroll over your needs with what matters to them. Assert yourself and be confident in the fact that you too deserve a seat at the table. Know that you can do anything that anyone else can do, if not more. This is about treating yourself as an equal. No more putting others before you and above you, from now on you put them beside you because you matter just as much. Taking up space is about restoring the balance. You are no longer people pleasing to avoid conflict or worrying about inconveniencing others with your voice. You are finally taking up the space that you are entitled to and reminding everyone that you are equally as important. Take up space.

STOP TRYING TO FIT IN

Your goal isn't to try and fit in. You were not put on this earth to change the person you are so that you fit into someone else's mold. Your goal is to be this incredible, real, wonderful and authentic version of yourself. You are not supposed to be like anyone else. You are who you are, embrace it. You have to be brave enough to say *'This is who I am and this is how I choose to live. Take it or leave it. Either way I will be fine.'* You can't dilute who you are in the hope that it makes other people like you more. That would be such a waste of *who you are*. The authentic version of you deserves *full* recognition, *full* love and *full* support but you will only get that if you stop altering yourself to fit in. Be proud to be you.

YOU DO NOT NEED ANYONE ELSE'S APPROVAL

You don't need the approval of anyone else in order to feel good about yourself. You don't need anyone else to think you are capable, beautiful, lovable or good enough for all of those things to be true. Sometimes we give our worth away by hoping that others like us and find value in us, because only then will we allow ourselves to find value in ourselves. The value and love you have for yourself needs to be totally independent of what others think of you. You have been waiting for others to choose you, when in fact what you really need is to *choose yourself*. It's time that you learnt to love yourself unconditionally and accept yourself as worthy and enough. Because the validation you are looking for from other people must come from *you* instead. You are everything you need to be already and no one's disapproval can take that away from you.

YOU ARE SELF-MADE

Everything that you are is a result of everything that *you* built. You are self-made. You built yourself. It was you who wanted better for yourself and then did the work to grow to where you are now. It was you who picked up the broken pieces and put them back together, one by one, to form the magnificent person that you are today. You took everything that you faced and turned it into something spectacular. You built yourself from the ground up despite all the opposing forces and challenges. Be proud of that. That was all *you* and no one can take that away from you. Never underestimate how much strength it took for you to become who you are now. Never again think that you are not capable of doing big things, you have *already done* big things. You overcame everything. You are remarkable.

THERE IS NOTHING WRONG WITH YOU

Stop giving yourself such a hard time. There is nothing wrong with you. Things are going better than you realize. You are absolutely fine as you are. You are being way too self-critical and you need to give yourself a break. When you look at your life, you look at it so zoomed in that every single small detail of your life looks worse than it is. It's really not that bad and you are doing *much* better than you think. Your life is amazing, and you are far too harsh on yourself. You are not broken, you are not behind and you are not doing life wrong. Your life is perfectly normal and more similar to everyone else's then you realize. We often forget that life is crazy, it throws curveballs at you and it's not as straightforward as we all imagined it to be - and that applies to *everyone*. Don't let the natural ebbs and flows of life make you sprint to the conclusion that there is something wrong with you. *There really isn't.*

ALWAYS BUILD YOURSELF UP

You are so *incredibly* powerful. Your words are powerful and your beliefs are powerful. But you have to use this power to build yourself *up* rather than tear yourself down. You can convince yourself of anything, absolutely *anything* so make it something good. Start being kinder to yourself. Be committed to bringing the best out of yourself, to building up your confidence, nourishing your self-love, telling yourself you are worthy and being grateful for yourself and your life. Be dedicated to interrupting negative thoughts about yourself and instead show up for yourself in a positive way time, after time, after time. Ask yourself, does this thought, behavior, or situation make me feel good about myself? If the answer is no, well then it is self-sabotage and something *needs* to change. You are so powerful and if you would just use that power for good to build yourself up and make yourself feel as incredible as you deserve to then you would become truly unstoppable.

REMEMBER WHAT YOU BRING TO THE TABLE

Everyone is so quick to tell you what they bring to the table, what they can offer and how important they are. People are so good at making it all about them that it is easy to forget how significant *you* are and how much value *you* add too. Don't let yourself feel small in the presence of others, you are their equal in *every* way. Remind yourself that *actually,* you bring a truckload to the table too. You *also* have so much to offer. Remind yourself that you can equally match them, if not exceed. You get to take up space too. The qualities you have and the value you bring does not get watered down by someone else's qualities and value. You are not less and they are not more. You deserve a seat at that table just as much as they do. The second you forget this you will start to feel inferior. You are *never* inferior, and no one can make you feel inferior but you. You are *everything* and more. Remember that.

NO ONE GETS TO DECIDE WHAT YOU ARE WORTH

Know your worth *undoubtedly* and stop waiting for other people to make you feel like you are good enough. You do not need the validation of another person in order to feel worthy - no one else gets to decide what you are worth. *Ever.* You are worthy with or without their approval and you owe it to yourself to never forget that. The truth is when you base your self-worth on someone else's opinion of you, they will always conclude that you fall short in some way. Not because you aren't good enough, but because their own insecurities don't want to see you shine too brightly. This is why listening to the negative judgment of others is pointless, it is driven by other people's *own* self-worth issues and isn't a true reflection of who *you* are. It is *your* job to protect your view of yourself. Never let anyone make you feel inferior, unworthy or lacking. *You lack nothing.* Take ownership of your self-worth and realize that feeling worthy, loved, valued and whole is totally and purely based on the relationship you have with *yourself.*

YOU CAN BE CONFIDENT

You can be confident. The biggest mistake you can make is thinking that because you aren't confident or haven't been very confident before that you can't ever be. You can. But confidence is **taken**, not given to you. Confidence is taken by slowly pushing yourself out of your comfort zone. Confidence is taken when you decide that you deserve to feel strong, powerful and to be heard. Confidence comes when you push yourself a little further than you have ever been willing to push before. Confidence comes when you nurture yourself and realize that you deserve the very best from life. You will earn your confidence bit by bit each time you let yourself step into the limelight and take up space. How much longer are you going to let your lack of confidence take opportunities from you, what are you waiting for? Confidence is yours to take – *so go and take it.*

STOP SHRINKING YOURSELF TO MAKE OTHER PEOPLE FEEL COMFORTABLE

This is your reminder to stop shrinking *yourself* to make *others* feel comfortable. You do not need to hold back or play it small just to make sure that other people don't feel threatened by you. Never shrink your achievements, intelligence, voice or opinions just so that others don't feel you are shining too bright. You owe it yourself to do big things, take up space and have your voice heard. Remember, it is not your problem if others find themselves intimated by who you are. You need to show how outstanding you really are and what you have to offer the world and if someone doesn't like it then that's on them. You can't let people in your life who *feel limited*, in turn *limit you*. Stop shrinking yourself, stop playing small, let the world see what you have got to offer.

DON'T BELIEVE EVERYTHING YOU THINK

Your mind is going to play tricks on you sometimes. It's going to tell you how bad things are going, how much you messed up, that you are not doing well enough, that you are not loved and a whole range of other lies. But you can't believe everything you think because it simply isn't true. Sometimes your insecurities get a little rowdy and tell you utter nonsense and when that happens you have to push back and talk some sense into yourself. Your thoughts will run wild if you don't control them and part of controlling them is not believing everything you think. Interrupt the negative self-talk and reframe it to something better. Get into the habit of questioning what you are thinking. Change the narrative, rewrite your thoughts and *choose* better ones. Is there any real evidence at all for the criticisms you are telling yourself or are you just letting your emotions run wild and things aren't as bad as you think?

YOUR WORTH IS NOT DICTATED BY YOUR ACCOMPLISHMENTS

Dear overachiever, you need to hear this: Your worth is not dictated by your accomplishments. *Yes,* you are doing amazing things and *yes* that's great. But there is *so much more* to you than that. You cannot pin every inch of your self-worth to your accomplishments because the two are not correlated. Your worth has absolutely nothing to do with what you achieve. You are worthy *regardless*. Your default setting is worthy and you cannot earn more worth by achieving more. You can overachieve as much as you want to but understand that it won't change a thing. You don't need to *do more* in order to *be more*. There is so much more to you than your goal list and you are good enough even if all of your achievements vanished tomorrow. You are and always have been worthy and enough just as you are.

DON'T ABSORB THE NEGATIVE

Let's cut to the point. Not everyone is going to like you, people will judge you, people will comment on you and some of it is not going to be nice. But so what? Let them dislike you. Let them think what they want to think. Why would that ever matter to you? The only thing that matters in all of this is that you protect *your view of yourself.* Don't let anyone convince you that you are inferior or lacking in any way. You are absolutely not. You cannot absorb the negative views, comments or opinions that others have of you. No matter what, you cannot let someone's opinion of you affect how you view yourself. Your confidence and self-esteem belong to *you* and other people do not get to affect them. So, let all the bad things people have to say slide right off you like butter on a hot day. You are incredible regardless of what anyone thinks.

YOU HAVE TO BELIEVE IN YOURSELF

You have to believe in yourself wholeheartedly and leave no room for doubt. We live in a world where no one is going to care if you believe in yourself or not. No one is going to come and make you feel better or tell you that you are good enough and no one is going to push you to make you succeed. It all has to come from *you*. Believing in yourself is a decision. It is deciding that if anyone can do it it's you. Regardless of your past track record, regardless of your doubts, regardless of your fears. You have decided to back yourself and to trust yourself to find a way to succeed. You can't always dictate that you will succeed the first time, but what you can dictate is that you will have the resilience and grit to get up, dust yourself up and keep going until you get there. You have to go *all* in. Give it everything you've got. No more playing from the side lines, watching from the outskirts and hoping you get your shot. Step into your greatness, *even* if it terrifies you. Start thinking that the *best-case* scenario *can* happen for you. Because at the end of it all, it won't matter how many times you failed, all that will matter is that you gave yourself a chance. Belief is a decision, and you need to decide that you are worth your best shot.

PEP TALKS FOR SELF-LOVE

SELF-LOVE IS UNCONDITIONAL

Somewhere along the way you decided that the love you have for yourself is conditional. That you are only worthy of self-love on the condition that you ticked certain boxes. Maybe it was how you looked, what you achieved, who you pleased or any other criteria that you have decided somehow would make you *enough*. Somewhere along the way, the love you have for yourself became *dependent* on things. But this is *not* how self-love works at all. Self-love is *unconditional,* it is without conditions, criteria or requirements. There are no boxes you need to tick; you are worthy and good enough *as you are*. It's time that you start to love yourself as a whole and not just the parts of yourself deem good enough. Accept that you are a 'work in progress' - *we all are* - and see your value *as you are*, flaws included. Your problem has never been your worth, your problem is that you have failed to recognize how *abundantly* worthy you already are.

YOU SHOULD BE PROUD OF YOURSELF

You are so busy focusing on where you are going that you haven't stopped to notice how far you have come. Take a moment to stop and acknowledge the difference you have made in your own life. It wasn't easy but *you* did it. If you look back even a few years, it is astonishing how much growth and progress you have made. Take it back even further and the results are incredible. That was all you - no one else did that for you. You should be proud of yourself, your life is remarkable. So often you are too busy worrying about the next thing you want to achieve to stop and realize what you have *already* done. Be proud of yourself for who you are today, you have come so far. So take a moment to look back and enjoy the view.

VOWS

When you get married you make a vow of *unconditional* love to another person. A vow to love them throughout the good times *and* the bad. A vow to be by their side no matter what and regardless of how mad with them you are. You vow to have permanent compassion for them and to accept them not only at their best but also at their worst. You make life altering vows and commit to unwavering love for another person. Yet when it comes to how you love yourself, *rarely* do you offer the same dedication. One false move and you judge yourself, doubt yourself and question your worth. You struggle to be kind yourself, struggle to forgive your mistakes and fall *in and out* of self-love. Don't you think it's about time that you started making those big meaningful vows to yourself? Vow to stand by yourself for better or for worse. Vow to never give up on yourself. Vow to forgive yourself and to be loyal to yourself when times get hard. Remember, you signed up for *both* the happy days and the sad days with yourself. The days where you like yourself and the days that you don't. You have to make a vow to love yourself unconditionally even when that is the last thing you want to do. Because really, *you* are who you are spending the rest of your life with no one else.

TREAT YOURSELF RIGHT

How can you begin to expect other people to treat you right if you don't even treat yourself right? *It starts with you.* You set the tone of how you want to be treated and it begins with how you view, speak to and treat yourself. Speak to yourself nicely, put *your* needs first, think good thoughts about yourself. Nourish yourself properly: good food, good sleep, exercise, rest and fulfillment. Invest in yourself and your wellbeing. Treat yourself like your most prized possession, because you quite literally are the best thing you own. Have care and compassion for yourself. In doing all of this you will raise the bar and only accept other people treating you well too. The first love is self-love, it underpins all the other love in your life. Until you get your self-love right you will not demand the right level of love from other people in your life. The way you treat yourself sets the standard that you are willing to accept from others. *It all begins with you.*

THE END OF SELF-SABOTAGE

This here marks the end of self-sabotage, *never again* will you turn on yourself and pull yourself apart. *Never again* will you speak poorly of yourself. *Never again* will you doubt yourself, criticize yourself or be hard on yourself. *Never again* will you treat yourself as though you are unworthy. *Shut. That. Right. Down.* There is no space for that in your life. From here on out, vow to work with yourself and *not* against yourself. Vow to cheer for yourself, love yourself, value yourself and believe in yourself. Self-sabotage has *never* rewarded you - it has always held you back and stood in your way. Times are changing for you now. Going forward you are going to embrace *every* part of who you are. You are going to care for yourself and love yourself *unconditionally*. You will eliminate any form of negative self-talk and instead bathe yourself in words of encouragement and kindness. *You* are your closest ally and starting now you will act like it. It is time to be with one yourself and love yourself deeply.

FORGET PERFECT

Chasing perfection is like dedicating your life to unicorn hunting. You are going to spend a lot of time searching for this mythical beast that doesn't exist and eventually look back on your life and wonder why you ever wasted so much time on it. When the goal is perfection our thinking becomes very rigid, we decide that we are either *good enough* or *not* depending on whether we have ticked off an impossible list of perfect criteria we have set for ourselves. But what if we learnt to accept and celebrate our imperfections instead? In Japan they have the term Kintsukuroi which means 'golden repair'. When a piece of pottery breaks, they repair it with gold which acts like glue to piece it back together again. As a result each piece of repaired pottery has unique imperfections which make it even more beautiful, desirable and rare - *a one of a kind*. Everything that makes you different, every quirk, every opinion, every scar is like a brush stroke to a masterpiece. If you start looking at things with a different perspective, maybe those flaws aren't as bad as you think, maybe they are gifts which make you more unique. No one else will ever be you, you are one in a million and you owe it to yourself to value that.

TAKE A COMPLIMENT

Take the compliment, let it soak in and enjoy it. Why are you always so quick to brush off nice things that are said about you? You wonder why you sometimes don't feel great about yourself, is it really any surprise when you are so quick to remember all of the criticism and the unkind words but not the good stuff. *Take the compliment.* Absorb all the good things said about you, the nice words, the praise, the recognition for the wonderful person you are. Filter out anything negative and only absorb the things that remind you of how great you are. From now on you are going to really let yourself feel *good* about yourself. You are going to relish the fact that it is you that is being praised, be flattered that it is you who is being noticed and realize that *you* are highly valued. Bask in it! Let yourself feel every ounce of goodness that comes your way and *slam dunk* any negative thing said about you straight in the trash where it belongs.

REGARDLESS OF THE SEASON

Regardless of whatever season you are experiencing in your life, a good one or a bad one, you *have* to love yourself. It's easy to love yourself in a good season, when things are going well and when life feels good. But there are going to be some particularly tough seasons in your life when it feels harder to love yourself. It is so easy to abandon yourself when things get difficult, to be hard on yourself, blame yourself or decide that because things are tough you are not worthy of love. Seasons in your life will change, but the love you have for yourself *cannot*. You can't turn on yourself when things get tough. You have to love yourself despite the fact that you are going through a tough season. It is in these tough seasons that you need to be dedicated to having love for yourself regardless of how your life looks. Your self-love has to be unconditional, you have to vow to never give up on yourself and *see that vow through*. You are worthy when life is good. You are worthy when life is bad. Regardless of the season, you always will matter.

BODY CONFIDENCE

You need to understand this: Your body is absolutely beautiful *exactly* as it is. It's time that you started to see that and appreciate your body the way that it *deserves*. There is no such thing as the perfect body or the perfect way to look. You aren't supposed to look a certain way and your body is not worth any less because it doesn't fit the idea of perfect beauty standards. Not even the models in magazines look like the models in magazines, they are airbrushed and retouched so that they look like something that doesn't exist naturally. So please don't waste your incredible body by hating the fact that it doesn't look like someone else's. Your body is *not* the problem and *never* has been the problem, the problem is you have convinced yourself that it needs to be different in order to be good enough. You look better than you think you do, you just need to stop giving yourself a hard time and instead realize that you can feel good in your body right now *as you are.*

KNOW YOUR WORTH

Stop benchmarking your self-worth against things that have no relation to your worth at all. You are not your weight, job, ability, or achievements. You are not your relationship, salary, parents or your past. You are so much more than all of that and those things *do not* define you. Yet often you struggle to accept yourself fully because there are things on this list (and more) that don't fit into your definition of 'perfect' or 'enough'. There is nothing you need to prove, do, or change in order to be enough or worthy. You are already enough, you are whole, complete, adequate and worthy already. So please, instead of looking for things you can add to your life to make you more worthy, realize that you will not find anything externally to increase your worth. You are completely worthy already, it's time you let yourself realize that.

YOUR LIFE ISN'T SUPPOSED TO LOOK LIKE ANYONE ELSE'S

Before you panic because your life looks so different to those around you, I want you to remember this: Your life isn't *supposed* to look like anyone else's. No two lives are comparable, and we simply are not supposed to be on the same path as everyone else. Our lives and the lives of others are totally separate journeys are they are *supposed to be different*. We are on our own path, and they are on theirs. You aren't *on* or *off* track in life, neither are they. Because there isn't actually anything that you should be doing in your life right now. There is no criteria or list of things you should be ticking off. There is no stage of progression you should be reaching right now. Instead, your life is your own and it is supposed to be stunningly unique and different. You are doing it right by just doing it *your way*. You are on the right path because you are on *your* path. Celebrate that you are not on the same path as others, because that means you have followed what is right for *you*.

DON'T BE SO HARD ON YOURSELF

Don't be so hard on yourself. The inner criticism, the harsh judgment and the self-doubt, it's *got* to stop. You are doing so much better than you think and your life is so much more incredible than you realize, but you have to let yourself enjoy that and stop putting so much pressure on yourself. Every single one of us gets it wrong at points. You are ok to make mistakes, you are ok to have flaws and you are ok to want better for yourself, but that doesn't mean you get to be so harsh on yourself. You deserve to be treated well and with the respect you deserve, not just by other people, but most importantly by yourself. Don't dull your own light by picking yourself apart, doing so will set the tone for your whole life and you deserve so much better than that. Your job is to bring out the best in yourself and stand a better chance of doing that by being kind to yourself. You may not be where you want to be *but that is ok*, you are doing great, and your life is worthy regardless of where you are on your journey.

YOU ARE ENOUGH

You *are* enough, you *have always* been enough, and you *will always* be enough. Nothing will ever change that. But what does have to change is how you see yourself. You do not need to do any more or be any more to be worthy. Your worth is not based on how you look, what you earn, who you please, the people you know or how much other people like you. You are enough purely based on the fact that *you exist,* and nothing is ever going to change that. You are the whole package *as you are*. Your opinions *matter*, who you are *matters* and everything you need is within you already.

DON'T COMPARE YOUR LIFE TO ANYONE ELSE'S

Before you give yourself a hard time about where you are in your life compared to everyone else, please remember this: We are all human, having a human experience which is filled with highs and lows. Just because you can't see other people's challenges doesn't mean they aren't there. You don't see their hard days, their struggles, their mistakes or their rejections. You don't see their heartbreaks, failures, fears and insecurities. You see what they *want you to see* and that is never the full picture. So before you compare and conclude that there's something wrong with you for not having a perfect life, please know that *no-one* has a perfect life. Be kind to yourself, you are doing better than you think.

BELIEVE IN YOURSELF

You haven't got any other option. You absolutely *have* to believe in yourself. Believe to the very core of your being that you are capable of anything, *because you are*. Before you tell me that it's not that easy, that you can't just flip the switch and believe in yourself, I want you to know this: Your mind will believe *anything* you tell it and you have spent far too long telling yourself that you can't when you *can*. Are you really going to live your whole life letting some made up doubt dictate your path? No, you are absolutely not. You are going to start over from today and decide that there is absolutely nothing that you cannot do. You are going to rewrite the script and start telling yourself that you are brave, worthy, incredible and can handle *anything* that comes your way. No one's going to come and remove your doubt for you, that's not how the world works - this one's on you. You have to believe in yourself.

FOCUS ON YOU

Life is *not* a spectator sport, and your life cannot be improved by watching what others are doing with theirs. Your focus has to be on *you*. You are the main event in your life and when you forget this you let comparison take away all of the happiness and pride that you deserve to feel about your own journey. There is no way you can make the most of the opportunities in front of you if you are too busy focusing on someone else and what *they* are doing. How will watching someone else succeed in their life change your life in any way? *It won't.* There is no correlation, they are two separate events. What if instead you turned all the focus onto all of the incredible aspects of your *own* life. Your life is incredible, and it is your journey that matters most.

IT'S OK IF YOUR LIFE DOESN'T LOOK LIKE YOU EXPECTED IT TO

It's ok if your life doesn't look like you expected it to by now. The truth is most of us are not living the life we expected to be living. We make the mistake of thinking that we can plan our whole lives out, and then expect it all to go *exactly* to plan. But that isn't how life works. So is it really any surprise that our life's look a little different to what we expected? The reality is that life is messy and comes with twists and turns that you could never have predicted. You planned for the perfect life but life itself is not perfect. Although your life may look different to what you expected it doesn't mean it's any less of a success. Your life is full of so many achievements and incredible moments and you should be so proud of who you are and how far you have come. Do not discredit it because it is not exactly what you had planned. Go easier on yourself because you are doing so much better than you think. So many of your greatest moments so far were never in your plans, so life being different to what you expected is not necessarily a bad thing. Life is always surprising you with something new and incredible that you could have never predicted. So be kinder to yourself, this is exactly where you should be right now.

PEP TALKS TO GUIDE YOU THROUGH UNCERTAINTY

YOU WILL ALWAYS FIND YOUR WAY

Sometimes life will derail you and make you feel totally blown off course. There will be moments in your life where you feel completely overwhelmed and as though you have lost your way. In these moments, I need you to remember that you can never actually lose yourself and that no matter what you *will always* find your way again. No matter what you face and no matter how big the challenge is, nothing can ever shake you up to the point where you are lost forever. You will *always* come back to yourself. You will always reconnect to your roots; you will always remember who you are and get yourself back on the path you belong. You can never truly lose yourself, that is the one constant in your life. You will always be rooted to who you are. It's going to be ok; you will land on your feet and things will settle down again. That is the one guarantee - you will always find your way.

SEE WHERE IT GOES

Sometimes change can be scary. You have no idea what's going to happen or where it will go. But that's exactly the point, you never know where those next steps are going to take you. Change can take you to the most amazing people, places and experiences. Change can lead you to opportunities, beautiful moments and peace. Change can give you everything you have ever wanted. So, before you worry about what's happening in your life just wait and see where it goes. You never know what magical chapter of your life is waiting just around the corner.

NO ONE SAID IT WOULD BE EASY

Guess what. No one said it would be *easy*, it's not supposed to be *easy,* and you were kidding yourself if you expected it to be *easy*. That's not how this works, success is *not* easy. Growth is *not* easy, and progress is *not* easy. Whenever we get started with something we are always guilty of simplifying it in our heads. We picture things going perfectly, we don't foresee obstacles that were always going to be part of the journey and we aren't realistic about what it really takes to achieve big things. Doing big things with your life is *not* easy and if it was then it wouldn't be a big deal, everyone would do it and it wouldn't be extraordinary. The bigger the goal the harder it is. But that's not a bad thing. The hard you are feeling right now is your fight for better. If what you are facing right now is tough and uncomfortable then that's *good*. It means that you are pushing for something bigger. Bigger than your fears, bigger than your comfort zone and bigger than anything you've ever done before. Trust me, it is so much better to take on things that change you for the better, than to take the easy route and never really see what you are capable of.

JUST TAKE IT ONE STEP AT A TIME

Stop thinking that you need to have it *all* figured out in order to get started, you definitely don't. Just start - even if it feels like a complete mess at first, just get off the start line. Nothing holds you back as much as *never* actually starting. Just take it one small step at a time, that's all you need to do. Don't worry about the bigger picture, the bigger picture will fall into place on its own. Just take the first logical step, *and then* the next *and then* the next. You don't need to go charging after the end goal today and you simply don't have to focus on everything all at once. Break it down, bit by bit into manageable chunks until eventually the path will become clear. You don't attempt to climb a whole staircase in one go, you know you will get to the top far quicker by taking it stair by stair. Focus on taking small steps in the right direction, because those small *but significant* steps will all add up and create huge shifts in your life.

DO IT AFRAID

If you don't control your fear, your fear *will* control *you*. It is as simple as that. So sometimes you just *have* to do it afraid. Do it even if you are terrified. Do it even if your stomach churns and your knees knock. Do it even if you don't feel ready and you feel way out of your depth. Because when you *do* take that leap you will realize that the whole time you were *more* capable than you thought. That actually, you were *far more* ready than you let yourself believe. Your fear gets it wrong a lot, it underestimates you and it's only when you go for it do you realize you were worthy of the challenge the whole time. Whatever it is, whatever you truly want for yourself *just do it.* There is no shame in being afraid, that's part of life. Fear never really goes away and so you have to do what you want to do *despite* your fear. Take the leap and do it afraid.

LET GO OF THE OUTCOME

It's really not all about the outcome in the end. The outcome is not the main event, it's the journey that matters. It's the journey that makes up most of your life. That is where most of your time will be spent and so you need to let yourself enjoy it. Yes the end goal is important - but there is so much life that has to be lived and enjoyed *before* you reach the end goal. Take it day by day and let yourself enjoy the journey as you go. Be in the present moment and enjoy whatever today brings without worrying about what comes next. Do the absolute best you can but know that ultimately what will be will be. All you really have is right now.

LIFE NEVER GIVES YOU MORE THAN YOU CAN HANDLE

If it all feels too much right now, then I want you to remember this: Life will never give you more than you can handle. Even when you feel like giving up, even when nothing makes any sense and you feel like you are at your limit - know that life will *never* give you more than you can handle. You will survive whatever it is you are facing right now; you can handle it and it is *not* too much for you. As hard as this may be you cannot quit on yourself, you cannot give up and you cannot stop fighting. Life challenges you because it's trying to grow you, it knows you have more to give and pushes you to expand and become stronger. It challenges you so that you can really understand *who you are* and what matters to *you*. But to grow you, it needs to take you close to your limit so that you are forced to dig deep and bring that remarkable strength buried deep inside you to the surface. There is always purpose in your pain and even if it doesn't make sense right now, know that one day it will. Realize your own strength. This won't end you. This won't defeat you. This won't stop you. You can survive anything that comes your way.

IF YOU FEEL STUCK

Feeling stuck is a good thing. It means you have outgrown where you are, and you are ready for more. You may *feel* stuck in life, but you never actually *are* stuck. Feeling stuck is simply that, *a feeling*. Whereas actually at any point and at any moment, you can make moves that will change your circumstances and move you to where you want to be. You are *not* stuck, you are just so swept up in the feeling that you are struggling to see solutions. Deep down you know what your next move is, and you know what needs to change. If you feel stuck right now, make one small change to your life. *Any change.* Even the smallest move in the right direction will create a ripple, and eventually, that ripple will become a wave, and in turn it will transform your whole life. You can redesign your whole life in tiny bite-sized chunks, you don't need to overwhelm yourself in order to move mountains, you just need to start. You are *not* stuck.

YOU HAVE TO TAKE THE RISK

If you know you could be *happier,* if you know that you need *more* from your life then you *have* to take the risk. Nothing is ever risk-free, life is always risky no matter what you do. It's risky to stay where you are and settle for less than you want, and it's risky to go after it *all* and potentially experience challenges and failure. So if you are going to be risking it anyway, you may as well go for the risk that could *actually* give you a payoff and make you happy. It's a calculated risk because you know that no matter what comes your way you are going to figure it out and navigate through. So it is less of a risk than you think. Trust yourself to make something amazing of your life regardless of what comes into your path. You were not put on this earth to live half-heartedly. Rather, you deserve the best from life and that's what life will give you - *If you would just let it*. Be brave, you have to take the risk.

TRUST YOUR GUT

No one knows what is best for you more than *you* do. You know when something is right for you, and you know when something doesn't fit. You know what will make you happy and what will move you forward. Other people may have an opinion on your life, but they don't know you like you know yourself. Trust *your* gut and follow your own instincts and intuition. You have all the answers within you already, you just need to drown out all of the outside noise and start trusting your *own* thoughts, your *own* opinion and your *own* gut feeling. You know more than you think you do, and you can trust yourself to make the right decisions for your life.

YOU ARE NOT LOST

If you are feeling lost in life right now, then I want you to know that actually feeling lost is a sign that you are *exactly* where you are meant to be. I know that might not make sense but feeling lost and directionless is actually a sign of progress. It is a sign that you have outgrown your current life and circumstances, and you are ready for *more*. It is a sign that you are entering a period of massive growth in your life and that better things are on their way. That no-man's land feeling that you are experiencing is your soul searching for its next evolution. You are being nudged forward to something bigger and better and you have to grab it with both hands. You may feel derailed right now but know that this is a period of transition for you, you are changing course for a better destination. Feeling lost is a crucial part of rediscovering who you are. You are finding yourself, shedding old skin and *flourishing*. This is a new beginning and will take you to where you need to be, this is the storm that clears the path for you and will allow things to fall into place. You are not lost, you are in fact, *exactly* where you are meant to be.

YOU CAN'T CONTROL EVERYTHING

Relax, you can't control everything. Sometimes you need to go with the flow and trust that you will figure it out as you go. Let go of your need for control and feeling like you need to have all the answers. The reality is it is impossible for you to actually have all the answers. You can't control life completely. Life is unpredictable and is *supposed* to be unpredictable, so you need to get comfortable with not knowing what's going to happen next. Otherwise, you will waste so much time and energy trying to control things that you actually can't control at all. Letting go of control makes space for opportunities, great things will try to come into your life but when you are trying to control everything so tightly, you will ignore these great things and opportunities as they aren't in your tightly controlled plans. *Go with the flow*, let things be fluid and flexible and navigate as you go. You can handle whatever comes your way.

YOU DON'T NEED TO FEAR UNCERTAINTY

Uncertainty can feel overwhelming and scary, but I want to reassure you that you don't need to fear it. For you, uncertainty is a great thing. Uncertainty means that nothing is set in stone yet. Thanks to uncertainty you have the power to carve out your future to make it exactly what *you* want it to be. Uncertainty is what brings you *adventure* - new experiences, new people, new places, new happiness. Yes, it can bring unexpected challenges *but at the same time,* uncertainty also brings unexpected lucky breaks, miracles, opportunities, victories and wow moments. It just depends on how you choose to look at it. Uncertainty means nothing is certain yet, which leaves the door wide open for *amazing* opportunities to come and find you. Uncertainty means that nothing is fixed and so *you* get to decide what comes next. Some of your best experiences that are yet to come will be born out of the same uncertainty that you fear. Decide that for *you,* uncertainty is a source of good, it's working *for you* and not against you to help create a life that surpasses and exceeds all of your wildest hopes and dreams. *Thank goodness* there is uncertainty.

WHAT'S THE WORST THAT CAN HAPPEN

What is the worst that could happen? No really, what is the worst thing that could happen? Because when you stop and think it through you realize that even in the worst-case scenario you would find a way to be ok. There is *always* a solution, and you have to trust that you will find it. *Everything* is figureoutable, *everything* is fixable and nothing is ever as bad as it seems. So why worry? Why not just go for it? Give it a shot. Have an adventure and see where it takes you. Realistically, the worst-case scenario rarely ever happens and if it did *you would be fine*. You would get up, dust yourself off and recover. You will *always* land on your feet and you will *always* be ok. Even if your fear tells you otherwise.

YOU ARE BRAVER THAN THAT

You are *braver* than you think and it's time you started realizing it. You are braver than your fears, you are braver than your self-doubt, you are braver than someone's opinion of you, you are braver than your insecurities, you are braver than any failure, you are braver than your heartbreaks. You are *fiercely* brave and *always* have been. It's time that you really stepped into your bravery and realized that nothing is too big for you to overcome.

SOMETIMES IT DOESN'T GO TO PLAN

Sometimes things don't go to plan and sometimes the journey you think you are going to carve out for yourself isn't what you end up with at all. Instead of panicking when this happens, realize this; you cannot plan every detail of your life because you have no idea what amazing things life has in store for you. You could have never predicted the amazing people, opportunities, places, adventures and experiences that life has lined up for you. You need to allow for life's surprises, serendipity and wonderful events that you could never have planned. In other words, you need to give up control and let yourself go with the flow. When you go with the flow and trust life to take you where you need to be, you will realize that actually there is so much more out there for you than you could ever imagine and that actually, *not* having a plan was the best plan of all.

FEAR IS GOING TO COST YOU

Remember that being fearful always comes at a cost to you and so you need to be honest with yourself about what you fear more. Do you fear doing the thing that scares you or do you fear wasting your chance to do what you wanted with your life more? Life ends the same way for all of us and there is no escaping that fact. But sometimes knowing that is enough to make you realize that you have *nothing* to lose. You really do only live once, this is your one chance to be who you want to be. So stop letting your fears steal the life you want from you. Rip the plaster off, face your fears and give yourself everything you have ever wanted.

NO MATTER WHAT HAPPENS

No matter what happens, no matter what comes your way, know that *you are going to be fine*. Life can be overwhelming sometimes and when it is you have to remind yourself that no matter what you are going to be ok. You are going to conquer whatever comes your way just like you always have. You have shown time and time again how resilient you are and how much strength you can pull out of yourself when you need it most. You have beaten everything that has come to defeat you, you have kept focused and positive even when you wanted to crumble. You have been knocked down seven times and gotten up eight. Hard things don't phase you anymore, challenges don't shake you like they used to. You have walked through the flames and risen from the ashes enough times to know without a single doubt that you will *always* be fine.

IN THE MOMENTS OF DOUBT

Remember that life's timing is always perfect, that nothing is a mistake and that things will *always* work out for you. We all want what we want *instantly*, but the reality is things take time and progress is still happening *even* if it's slow. Quiet the panicked voice in your head that is telling you it is all going wrong. It is *not* all going wrong. Know that everything does happen for a reason and if you don't believe that then look back at your life so far. You have faced hard things before and yet things have *always* worked out the way they were meant to work out for you. You have always landed on your feet and this time will be no different. Whatever challenge you are facing right now is temporary, this hard moment will eventually pass, and you will be happy. Life has always provided for you, you didn't have to chase, you didn't plan, and yet good things happened. That was life making sure you got what you needed. Trust life, trust the process and remember that there are so many great things waiting for you that you can't even imagine.

YOU ARE GOING TO HAVE TO PIVOT

The only predictable thing in life is that life *will be* unpredictable. It will chop and change when you least expect it and you will find yourself in places and positions that you never imagined. Be prepared to pivot. Accept and expect that you are going to have to adjust your plans and change your strategy from time to time. Things are going to come out of nowhere and rock you, *but that's ok*, you expected this, and you can handle whatever you have to face. It doesn't mean you have failed when this happens, *it is part of life*. So go easy on yourself and understand that at points it's going to feel like it is all going wrong, but I promise you it's not, it's just a sign that it's time to change strategy. No matter how big the curve ball is that life throws at you, you can navigate through it so long as you are willing to adapt. That's your secret weapon, be prepared to change course, be willing to pivot and think on your feet. But also, look for opportunities. That's the most fantastic thing about life being unpredictable, the unpredictability creates opportunities for you. There is good to be found in everything, but to find it you need to be willing to pivot.

PEP TALKS FOR TOUGH TIMES

YOU HAVE TO EXPERIENCE ALL OF IT

Something you have to accept about life is that it will give you the *full* spectrum. We will each have to face the good, the bad, the great and the awful parts of life. No one is exempt and everyone must go through this. As much as life is about happiness, it is also about the hard times too. It is the hard times that make the good times feel good and add meaning and depth to it all. So we have to experience *all* of it, the ups *and* the downs. There is no fast-forwarding past the bad bits and there is no cherry-picking just the good bits. But that's ok, it is part of having a human experience and everything you have to go through will shape you and grow you in its own way. Let yourself feel it *all*, take what it has to give and use that to add to your life in some way.

IT IS ALL GOING TO BE OK

I know it doesn't feel like it right now, but I promise you that this will *all* be ok. Whatever is going on for you right now is a lot for anyone to manage, but you will get through this just like you have gotten through *everything* you have faced so far. It is ok to feel anxious right now, it is ok to feel overwhelmed and unsure of what is going to come next. These are all expected feelings. But you have to stay focused on the fact that it will *all be ok in the end*. It will all work out and it will not always feel like it does right now. What you are going through now is temporary, this is just a season in your life. It is just *one* chapter. All tough situations *must* eventually come to an end, this one included, and better times *will* begin. Keep going.

WHEN YOU ARE FEELING LOW

Sometimes we *need* to crash and burn a little bit. We need to let all the messy and chaotic feelings come to the surface so that we can process them and let them out. These 'low points' act as a release. You are letting it all pour out of you, letting yourself feel what you need to feel so that you can eventually regroup and move on from this. It's a moment to wipe the slate clean and start again. There is nothing wrong with you for feeling like this, you are just riding the rollercoaster that is life. We all ride it, and sometimes it's really hard. Right now, you are in a dip and those big dips on roller coasters can rattle you, but remember after a dip there is *always* a rise. It will get better, you will get to the very top again. You will feel good, healed, happy and at peace with where you are in your journey. Low points are just small moments where you need to take it a little easier on yourself. They don't last forever, and this will all pass. But for now, you need to be kind to yourself and keep going, the rise is coming.

YOU ARE UNBREAKABLE

Life is tough but never forget *so are you*. You may stumble and fall a little along the way, but nothing can ever actually break you. You are unbreakable. You were built to survive hard things and you *will* bounce back from anything you face. You can already see this in yourself, things don't rock you like they used to, you've gotten braver, stronger and more resilient. The next time you are up against a challenge you have to tap into this strength and remember *who you are*. Remember how much you have overcome already and know that this time will be no different. Hold your head high, do what needs to be done and find a way to make any situation work for *you*. It doesn't matter how tough things get because *you* will always be tougher.

FINISH WHAT YOU STARTED

Of course you feel like quitting, it's getting tough, it's getting hard and it's getting uncomfortable. It's getting to the bit that no one likes, the bit where it feels easier to walk away and quit rather than stay and finish what you started. It is at this point that you have to remember what you promised yourself. When you started *you knew* it wasn't going to be easy, but also you knew it was going to be worth it. You were full of excitement for this chapter of your life and you promised yourself that you would see it through even when it got tough. You promised yourself that when the tough times came you would work harder, keep at it and focus on the end goal. You promised yourself that you wouldn't give in and that you would stick to the course because the win would be worth it in the end. Well, you are here at that hard part now. It's here where you step up and finish what you started. See it through to the very end and claim your victory like you promised yourself you would.

IT IS JUST A BLIP

It's OK. You are ok, and it is all going to feel ok in the end. What you are experiencing is just a blip. It's a small bump in the road, it's not going to derail you and its damage will be minimal. Don't overthink it, remember you were expecting to face blips along the way, blips are part of life, everyone faces them, and everyone feels like this when they happen. Remember that this is not final. It is all about the recovery, how are you going to choose to react to this? What good can you take from this? Learn what you need to learn from this blip, then get *straight back up*. Don't sit in this for longer than you need to. Dust yourself off, recover yourself from this quickly and *keep going*.

IT IS NEVER THE WORST-CASE SCENARIO

Your mind will always exaggerate how bad things are as a way to protect you and this makes things seem worse than they really are. When this happens it is your job to zoom out, add some context and see the situation for what it *really* is. The worst-case scenario is *never* the worst-case scenario, it never ends up as bad as you think it will be. *Everything* is fixable, *everything* can be worked out. You can recover from *anything,* and every situation can be turned into a positive. When things go wrong, step back and look for possibilities to turn it around, because there is *always* a way to turn the situation around. Sometimes there's nowhere to go but up, so up you go. Remind yourself that the worst-case scenario rarely happens, but the *best-case scenario* happens all the time. As much as things can go wrong, things go right a lot more often. Best case scenario *can* happen for you and when it does it will be phenomenal.

COMPARTMENTALIZE IT

Don't deal with everything all at once. Give yourself a break. Everything has a place and you don't need to deal with everything all in one go. That would far too much for you to carry. Instead, compartmentalize things in your life. Break it up, space it out, and let yourself have moments of peace where you don't think about it at all. It will be dealt with but in its own compartment of time. Outside of that slot, it really doesn't matter, and you are free to relax. So relax.

DON'T BE SCARED OF THE CHALLENGE

How you view the challenge matters more than the actual challenge itself. What really matters is your perspective. How are you going to view this? Something that is going to defeat you or something that *you* are going to defeat. That will determine the outcome. Challenges and roadblocks aren't a bad thing, the problem is when you perceive them as something that can stop you. What if you saw challenges as just part of the journey, small blips that do not have the power to derail you? What if you saw them as something that you simply need to work through and nothing more? What if you saw challenges as an exciting plot twist in your story, something that adds to the adventure and teaches you? Frankly, if challenges are inevitable and are going to happen whether you like it or not, then you may as well try and take something good from them. You will have more chances of succeeding if you see them for their possibilities rather than their limitations. *It's all about perspective.*

YOU CAN SURVIVE ANYTHING

You can survive anything. You can survive heartbreak, failures, big mistakes, rejections, loss, bad days, bad weeks, bad months. You can survive it all. These things might hurt, but they will not break you. Don't underestimate yourself and just how much you can handle. You can ride the turbulent waves and come out the other side better than when you started. Things will get easier than they are right now, but you just can't give up on yourself. There is more to your journey than this.

YOU ARE TOUGHER THAN ANYTHING LIFE THROWS AT YOU

Don't ever forget that you are tougher than *anything* life throws at you. You are going to face some challenges throughout your life - that much is inevitable. But when you do, remind yourself that you are so much tougher than whatever comes your way. You have to remember that no matter what comes your way you *will* get through it. It may be hard at the time, it may be really unpleasant and it may feel like it won't end. But it will. You will remain undefeated and no matter how many times you get pushed down you will always come back up fighting. Nothing can hold you down because you will *always* find a way.

SINK OR SWIM?

What is it going to be? Sink or Swim. Every time you face hardship you are given a choice. Will you let this defeat you or will you find a way to make this work? Sometimes we don't realize it is a choice, we are so bombarded with the challenges of adversity that we can't see any other way this could go but badly. There is *always* another way, there is good to be found in *every* situation. But to find it you need to *choose* to seek it out. You need to choose to swim rather than sink, you need to choose to find a way to make the most out of this and make it work for *you*. Choosing to swim in the face of adversity isn't always easy. Adversity is going to bring big waves that will try to pull you right under. It's in these moments you realize that actually you are *stronger* than you thought, more *capable* and *adaptable* than you ever knew. Your determination to survive will awaken something within you and show you just how undefeatable you are. Nothing is ever hopeless, there is a positive to be found in everything you just need to be brave enough to seek it out.

IT GETS BETTER

You are in the middle of it right now. Not quite the beginning, not quite the end. Right in the middle, right in the part where it feels the hardest and like it's never going to be over. It's in this moment that it is so important for you to remember that it *does* get better, it *always* gets better. Every challenge you have faced eventually came to an end, this time will be no different. I know it might not feel like it, but I can promise you that life is working *for* you, not against you. These hard parts are always temporary. Which means that at some point this moment will pass and you will be happy again. But for now, you have to hold on that little bit longer and keep pushing that little bit more. You have made it through everything that has come your way so far, and so you will make it through this too. Keep going because I promise you it will get better.

THE STRUGGLE LEADS TO THE WIN

Just because you are struggling at something doesn't mean you are failing at it. The struggle is not necessarily a bad thing. The life you build for yourself as a result of the setbacks that you have faced will far exceed anything you could have done *without* facing setbacks. Sometimes facing challenges is the best thing that could ever happen to you. When you get where you want to get, *and you will get there*, you will realize that it was the struggles you faced that led you to the win. Everything you are facing is building you to who you need to be, keep going.

GET BACK UP NO MATTER WHAT

Getting knocked down is inevitable, but it is *how* you react to getting knocked down that shapes your life. No matter what happens to you, you have to get back up. See the times you get knocked down as mere pit stops. Let them be over quickly and do not let them define you. In the moment you probably won't feel like you can recover, it is in these times that you have to promise yourself that no matter how hopeless the situation seems, you will be committed to finding a way to dig deep and keep fighting for the very best life for yourself. Wrestle with your mind until the only thought that is left is '*I will recover from this, nothing is too big for me*'. Get back up no matter what.

LIFE ISN'T ALWAYS FAIR

Life *isn't* fair. That is just the way it is. But it's up to you to figure it out and make something of it despite the circumstances you have been given. You've got to take responsibility for your life, regardless of what shape it is in right now and regardless of whether it is your fault or not. The task of making the most of your life will always sit with *you*. I get that it isn't fair, and I get that other people have had an unfair advantage and that it was all too easy for them in comparison. *But that changes nothing.* It's pointless wasting your time looking at everyone else trying to decide who got dealt the better hand and whether it was fair or not. Instead, focus on the *possibilities* that are available to *you*. The part of life that *is* fair is the fact that you get to dictate the perspective you have on your life and because of that the possibilities are endless for *you*. You can make your life *anything* you want it to be, regardless of how fair or not your circumstances are. Nothing can stop you.

THE CHALLENGE WILL BUILD YOU

You are being built right now. All of the challenges that you are facing right now are building you and shaping you into the person you want to be. You may hate what you are facing, but you have to realize that *this* is how you grow. You are going to conquer this and, in the process, this is going to force you to evolve and expand who you are. This is forcing you to climb to new heights, challenge your intellect and develop as a person. You are becoming more creative, more strong-willed, and more resilient. It's forcing you to crush any doubts or insecurities. It may feel like it is breaking you but actually it is *building you*. You fear the challenges that are in your path, but you are not realizing how much you *need* them. Each challenge is a rebirth, an opportunity to shed a version of you that you have outgrown and instead evolve into what you are truly capable of. This obstacle will pass and when it does you are going to be left with all of the growth it provided. Don't be scared of this challenge. You need this more than you realize.

BETTER DAYS ARE COMING

Things *always* get better, it's just the way it works. You might not feel it now, but I promise you that better days are coming for you. Tough times don't last forever, and this is no exception. One day it will all be so different for you, and this will be a distant memory. There will be a day when you wake up and you are genuinely happy and at peace with where you are in your life. You will have overcome whatever you are going through right now, and you will be grateful that you kept going. There is *always* a light at the end of the tunnel, and you are closer to reaching it than you think. Keep going and remember that the only way out of this is *through it* and every single day you are getting closer to the better days.

THE COMEBACK IS ALWAYS BIGGER THAN THE SETBACK

Have you ever stopped to think that maybe this setback is exactly what you needed? Only a setback can push you to new levels and force you to up your game in a way that *nothing* else could. Winning doesn't teach you much, but setbacks? Setbacks *build* you. Your comeback will always be bigger than your setback, *because* of your setback. You are going to bounce back, and when you do, you will use every single ounce of this setback to your advantage. Everything is a learning curve and because of that things only ever get *better*. So don't let these setbacks phase you, there is an advantage for you in this, and there is something for you to gain in every failure. You will recover from your challenges and when you do nothing will be able to stop you. Because the comeback is always stronger than the setback.

THIS DOES NOT DEFINE YOU

Remember, whatever you are going through in your life right now *does not* define you. It is easy to feel consumed and overwhelmed by your current circumstances, but make no mistake, whatever you are facing *does not define you or your life*. Your challenges do not define you, your failings do not define you and your mistakes do not define you. None of these things are permanent and you cannot lose your sense of self in them. You are so much bigger than all of those things. Protect the view you have of yourself, you are not your current circumstances and this moment is not indicative of your final destination, it is merely a pit stop along the journey that you will move on from. You are still going to become the person you want to be and live the life you want to live. You can go on and take your life in any direction you want to regardless of what your life looks like right now.

YOU CAN DO HARD THINGS

Remember that *you can do hard things*. You can do the things that scare you. You can do the things that feel too big, and you can face the unknown. Your fear is making you underestimate yourself and doubt yourself. But let's be clear, there is *nothing* you cannot do. There comes a point when you have to face the challenge head-on and do the 'hard thing'. The 'how' doesn't need to be clear right now, you just need to be committed to staying the course and figuring it out as you go. Hard *doesn't* mean it's impossible, it just means that you are going to need to grow yourself in order to conquer it. I am glad this is hard for you, I'm glad something is going to push you to dig deep and figure out how to grow. I am glad something is going to make you tap into new depths of your ability. This is what you need right now. You can do hard things.

PEP TALKS FOR THE RELATIONSHIPS IN YOUR LIFE

DON'T LET THEM FIND YOU WHERE THEY LEFT YOU

Don't let them find you where they left you. Pick yourself up. Dust yourself off, start again, set new goals and reach new levels. Prove to anyone who has ever doubted you that *they got it wrong*. Make big moves, change your life and upgrade every inch of yourself. Make sure that when you cross paths with them again you are not where they left you. Step up, reinvent yourself and exceed everyone's expectations of you, including your own.

SOME PEOPLE WILL NEVER BE WHO YOU NEED THEM TO BE

You are going to save yourself a lot of time and a lot of effort when you accept that some people will never be who you need them to be. You want them to become someone you can depend on and someone who treats you right. You want mutual respect, consideration, kindness and a sense of normality in the relationship. Although that all sounds so simple, ultimately you can't expect someone to become something that they are not. This is just not who they are, and they are *never* going to give you what you need. You expect more from them than they are capable of, and they are *always* going to fall short and leave you disappointed. So maybe it's time that you stop investing so much into a person who will never give you what you need in return, and instead make space for someone who *can*. It's liberating to finally understand why this hasn't been working. It's not you. *It's them.*

MIXED SIGNALS ARE CRYSTAL-CLEAR SIGNS

People show you exactly how they feel about you through their actions, words and how they make *you* feel. There is no such thing as a mixed signal. The lack of effort, letting you down, the times they 'forgot', these are all crystal-clear signals as to how much value you hold in their life. Make sure that you are not ignoring what they are showing you just because it isn't what you want to see. If they value you, they will show you that clearly. You are worth so much more than being an afterthought. You can't keep waiting and keep hanging on to something that isn't there. There comes a point where you need to stop wasting the love you have to give on people who will never give it back. These things should never be forced, when they are *right,* they are *right*, and when you need to force them to work they are simply not meant to be.

YOU CAN LIVE WITHOUT THEM

I know It doesn't feel like it right now but know that you *can* live without them. You can live without them *and* feel whole, happy and complete. Throughout life, we meet people and intertwine parts of our lives with theirs and when that ends it can feel as though we have lost something that we can't live without. Please understand that what you are feeling isn't the loss of *them*, what you are feeling is fear that you have lost parts of *you* that you found when you were with them. The truth is you don't actually need anyone else as much as you think you do. Everything that they made you feel, the joy, happiness, growth, purpose and love - that *all* came from you. *They* didn't give that to you, that *wasn't* from them. It was always inside you, always yours and will forever be yours. Their role, and the reason they crossed your path, was to coax out what was already inside you and bring it to the surface for you to enjoy. You didn't lose them, you simply gained more of you. They helped you find parts of yourself that you needed to find and now they have nothing more to offer you. You *can* live without them, because truthfully it was *never* about them, it was about you growing and evolving into the next version of yourself.

DON'T CHASE PEOPLE

Don't chase people, don't chase validation from others and don't chase love and affection. *Remember who you are.* You are priceless, you are precious, you are the main event, and you can never make someone else more important to you than you are to yourself. You are the priority always. The best thing you can do is let people lose you rather than spend your time trying to convince them to want you back. You are too worthy to chase them, too worthy to beg for someone else's care and attention. If they cannot see just how special you are, then maybe you were aiming a little too low when you decided you wanted them. Never chase someone, don't you ever forget that.

YOU ARE NOT GOING TO BE ALONE FOREVER

You are *not* going to be alone forever, that's just *not* going to happen. At the right time and with the right person, it's *going to happen for you*. You are going to meet your person and have your happily ever after and when that happens you are going to wonder why you ever worried so much. You are panicking right now, but you really need to have more *faith* in yourself and in life. This isn't the conclusion yet; you are still on your journey and you don't know what is waiting just around the corner for you. You haven't met everyone you're going to meet yet. You don't know what's next for you, so why would you panic and conclude that it's never going to happen for you? Be patient and keep your heart wide open for your person. But most importantly live your life to the fullest *with* or *without* that other person. Because *you* are the main event in your life, and you don't need anyone else to complete you.

NOT EVERYONE IS GOING TO LIKE YOU

Let yourself be disliked - not everyone is going to like you in life and that is absolutely more than ok. You don't *need* everyone to like you, in fact, it is impossible for *everyone* to like you. People are like art - we are subjective. Some will adore you, but for others, you won't be to their taste. But that's ok, some people simply aren't your people. Ultimately it doesn't even matter if you are disliked, your world will keep spinning *perfectly* whether someone chooses to like you or not. What does matter though, is how much you like yourself. Don't prioritize making sure other people like you over actually liking yourself. You are your *only* constant, you are the only person who has to have a good opinion of you. Make it your number one priority to like *yourself* and accept *yourself* fully. You have to ask yourself who are you living for? Are you living for yourself, or are you living for the approval of others? People not liking you really doesn't have the earth-shattering effect on your life like you think it does.

YOU ARE NOT TOO MUCH

You are not *too much*. There is no such thing as being too much. If someone claims you are 'too much', maybe what they really mean is that they feel like they are not enough in your presence. Remember, your goal is to live a *full* life and that means being authentic, speaking up for yourself, being excited about your life, having purpose, being brave, having an impact and giving *all* you have to give. If all of that accumulates in you being 'too much' then *great*. Why on earth would you want to aim for less? You are the full picture, you are everything you need to be and you can't change that for anyone else. If someone is not comfortable with the space you take up then that's on them. The answer isn't for you to become less, just to make them feel like more. If you are deemed too much for them, then they are *welcome* to go and find less elsewhere. **No one gets to dim your light.**

READ THE RED FLAGS

Red flags are *red flags* and you know it. You can clearly see that they are red. Not yellow, not blue and certainly not green. *They are red.* Yet you head on over to them and let them run riot in your life despite the flaming red warning. A red flag is a dead end. Whatever you think it's going to bring you, *it's not*. Red flags do not change their color, red flags do not evolve, red flags will *always* be red flags. We have all dabbled with a red flag at some point and not one of us has left unscathed, if you play with a red flag you are *always* going to get burnt. Save yourself the pain and walk away while you can. Ignoring the warning signs will only get you hurt. Protect your self-esteem, confidence and self-worth, because every time you dabble with a red flag *that i*s what pays the price. Don't destroy your own peace by pretending to be color-blind, instead start treating red flags like the steaming dumpster fire that they are.

ANOTHER PERSON'S OPINION OF YOU IS NOT FACT

Never forget, another person's opinion of you is not a fact. Let other people say and think what they want about you. It really doesn't matter. Not everyone is going to understand you, understand what you're capable of and understand your perspective. They are going to get it wrong about you. Let them, it makes no difference to your life. But the mistake you can't afford to make is believing that what someone else says or thinks about you is true. No one knows you like you know you. You know who you really are, and you can't let anyone's misjudged opinion take that away from you. Your value is your value regardless of what others think.

HEARTBROKEN BUT NOT BROKEN

Broken hearts will *always* mend. No matter how hard it is to believe that right now, you *will* heal from this, you *will* recover, and you *will* feel whole again. This will just be another memory that will eventually fade. One day it won't matter anymore, you will move on and you will let yourself love again. Remember love doesn't always end this way, there will be a day where it has a happy ending. You *are* going to get what you have been waiting for in love. You *are* going to meet the person who will make everything make sense. They will treat you right and make you realize that you were never asking for too much, you were just asking for it from someone who was never meant for you. The right person knows how to love you without being told, they are the perfect fit and show you how *easy* you are to love. Your person will find *you*, they are drawn to you like a magnet. Because what's yours will always find its way to you. You have not been broken by this heartbreak, you are just being redirected to something better.

YOU ARE NOT RESPONSIBLE FOR ANYONE ELSE

You need to remember that you are not responsible for anyone else. You are not responsible for other people's happiness, progress, stability or growth. You can't change other people's lives no matter how much they would like you to. *They* are the ones that need to do what they need to do for *themselves*. The reality is not everyone is going to do the work on themself that they need to and even though it's hard to step back, you need to remember that it isn't down to you to fix anyone else's life. This all sits with them. It is so liberating to remind yourself that each person is their own responsibility, and you don't need to walk on eggshells just to keep everyone else happy. Focus on yourself and your own happiness, you are not responsible for anyone apart from yourself.

WHOLE REGARDLESS OF YOUR RELATIONSHIP STATUS

Whatever way the chips land for you in *any* area of your life, it is your job to make the best of it and to *find* happiness within your circumstances. Even if you end up single for most of your adult life, your life would still be rich, meaningful, and full of love and fun. You would go on adventures, book amazing trips and meet the most incredible people as you go. You would make new friends, eat great foods, experience incredible moments and create memories. You would build an amazing career, pursue your dreams, challenge yourself and truly get to know and love who you are. The truth is, you don't need anyone else to have a great life. Your life will always belong to you, and it will be a full, happy and meaningful life *regardless* of your relationship status. Remember you are so much more than any relationship you could be in, you are not *half* looking for another person to make you *whole*. You are whole as you are.

LET YOURSELF BE JUDGED BY OTHERS

Being judged is inevitable, you are going to be judged by others and equally, *you* will judge people too. So if you are going to be judged regardless, then you may as well let yourself go and do the things that make you happy. It's not your job to please everyone with how you live your life. It's *your* life and the only person who needs to be ok with it is *you*. So let them judge you, let them come up with a whole range of opinions of you if that is really how they want to spend their time. But no matter what, don't let their opinions stop you. You cannot sacrifice your happiness for the opinion of others. It's your life, it's your show, you are the priority, not them. So live how *you* want to live, do what *you* want to do and feel good about it.

LOVE EXISTS

You need to know that *great* love exists, *healthy* love exists, *easy* love exists, *fair* love exists, and *happy* love exists. Just because you haven't experienced the beautiful side of love yet, doesn't mean it doesn't exist. It does, and it will one day be the love you experience too. One day you will forget all of the rough love, the bad love, the painful love because all you will have in your life is the beautiful kind of love. Great love exists and that's exactly what you will get so long as you don't let yourself settle for anything less.

YOU DESERVE BETTER

Recognize when you deserve better. If they wanted to make you feel loved and cherished, *they would.* If they wanted to make you feel safe and secure in the relationship *they would.* Their lack of action, poor communication and low effort is telling you that you are not a priority for them and that you deserve better. Understand that it is *not* a case of you not being good enough for them, it is a case of *them* not being good enough for you. You have done all that you could possibly do to make this work and now it is time to choose *yourself.* Stepping into your happiness comes with saying goodbye to those who never wanted the best for you. The most important thing you can do is have enough self-love and respect to not settle for people who don't see your worth. You only hurt yourself when you choose people who were *never* prepared to choose you back. You deserve better.

WHAT IT MEANS WHEN THEY DON'T TREAT YOU RIGHT

Have you ever thought that how someone treats you is more of a reflection on *them* than it is on you? It's so easy to blame yourself when someone doesn't treat you right, it is so easy to believe that in some way *you* are responsible for how *they* have behaved. It is easy to believe that maybe if you had given them *more*, done *more* or been *more* then maybe it would be different. Understand this, often how someone treats you has *nothing* to do with you. It is a reflection on them, not you and you cannot take blame for someone else's behavior. They failed, not you. Don't question yourself or your worth. You are enough, you are deserving of love and you have *nothing* to regret.

LOVE SHOULDN'T BE PAINFUL

Sometimes we mistake things for love. Things that aren't good for us but we want them to be and so we convince ourselves that it's fine, it's ok, *it's love.* But love shouldn't be painful, love shouldn't be inconsistent or dependent on you always doing things *their* way on *their* terms. Love should be equal, fair, consistent and easy. It doesn't come with conditions or require you to sacrifice parts of yourself. When it's love, *really love,* you do not need to change who you are to make it work, because when you have to do that the only person you are really making this work for is *them* and that's not love at all. A big part of your role in any relationship is to remember who *you* are, what *you* deserve and what *you* are worthy of. That means choosing yourself every time and knowing that protecting yourself is worth more than *any* relationship. The right person doesn't need to be told how to love you, they are your puzzle piece, and they slot into your life without tension or friction. Don't settle, *real love* is worth holding out for.

YOU CAN'T CHANGE OTHER PEOPLE

Understanding this is going to save you a lot of time, heartache and pain: You cannot change other people, nor is it your job or responsibility to change other people. At some point, you need to accept that they are just not compatible with you, and they will never be who you need them to be. There is no point in pretending otherwise. Not everyone has a place in your life and the sooner you are honest with yourself about those who don't belong there, the better it will be for you. I know you think that you could change them and help them to learn to treat you differently. But the truth is *you can't* and it's not your job either. What you are seeing is their true character. They know what they are doing to you, they know the hurt they are causing. They also know that they can get away with it because you aren't going to walk away. People very rarely change and any change that does happen has to come from them, *not you*.

LOVE IS NOT EARNED

Love is not something you need to earn. You do not need to prove to anyone that you are worthy of their love. If someone loves you, they love you for who *you are* not for what you can do for them. You deserve consistent, reliable, dependable and uncomplicated love and you will get that when you stop accepting *less* than that. You cannot force what isn't meant to be. Instead, you owe it to yourself to make space for someone who can love and treat you how you deserve.

STOP ACCEPTING THE BARE MINIMUM FROM OTHER PEOPLE

Put the bar *higher* and expect to be treated well. You are too good to accept being someone's afterthought, their second choice, their reserve option. The person they call when their *actual* plans fall through. The person they know will chase after the small drops of love and affection they give you. By accepting the bare minimum, you are letting people know that it is *ok* to give you the bare minimum. *You* set the bar. You deserve so much more than this, but you will only get more when you stop accepting the scraps that they give you. You get to choose who takes up space in your life, so choose people who are *worthy* of a position. You deserve to be someone's main choice, to take first place and to be made to feel like you *truly* matter. But for you to have that *you* need to set the tone and to stop accepting the bare minimum.

YOU OWE THEM NOTHING

Here is a reminder that you *do not* owe anyone anything. You are deserving of love, respect, kindness and peace *as you are*. You do not need to earn these things. Likewise, you do not need to feel guilt over being who you truly are, you have done *nothing* wrong, and you have nothing to feel shame about. Let me be clear, you do not need to apologize for who you are, you are not a burden and you *do not* need to change. Know that you are *allowed* to disappoint others, do this rather than disappointing *yourself*. You do not owe anyone any explanations for your life. You get to be who you want to be and feel how you want to feel without explaining it to make them happy. You owe them nothing.

THE PEOPLE IN YOUR LIFE WILL CHANGE

As you evolve as a person the people in your life are going to change and that is a good thing. The more you know your worth, the more self-love you have, and the more you know what you deserve, the more the people in your life will change and that is *more than ok*. There is no longer space in your life for unbalanced relationships. Not only will you want to move on from people, but they will want to move on from you too. The new you is different. You can't be manipulated any more, you can't be walked over, and you can't be used. You aren't the version of you that worked for *them* anymore. Part of your evolution is understanding that not everyone from your past chapters belongs in your future chapters. Some paths you have to walk alone *and that's ok*. Because it was never about anyone else. This has always been about you making the choices and decisions that are right for *your* life. Even if they are hard. Your circle will shrink, but you will have swapped *quantity* for *quality*. New people take their place. People who match your energy and elevate you to *greater* heights. Change is a good thing.

YOU NEVER NEEDED THEM

You didn't lose them. They lost you. You were the prize. You were the one worth keeping. You *can* and *will* survive without them. It might not be something you see right now but that doesn't change the fact that you *are* better off without them. You got so consumed with trying to make *them* happy, that you forgot that the person you really needed to prioritize was *you*. This is what you need to relearn now, you need to relearn making yourself a priority. This starts by realizing that you *never* really needed them, they *never* completed you, they *never* gave you anything that you didn't already have. The parts of you that you liked about yourself when you were with them *always* came from you. You were whole before them, and you are still whole after them. You have lost nothing by taking a step away from them. You are finally realizing your own worth and you are no longer willing to compromise on your happiness for someone else. The truth is you can't keep going back to things that were never meant for you in the first place. You may have *wanted* them, but you never *needed* them. Right now is about rediscovering who *you* really are and what *you* want for your life.

SOME FRIENDSHIPS WILL EXPIRE AND YOU NEED TO LET THEM

Some friendships will expire and that is absolutely ok. But when this happens you have to be honest with yourself because holding onto something that has run its course is not good for anyone. Sometimes things *need* to end, and you *need* to let them. It's a hard reality to face and so it can be tempting to drag out expired friendships long past their sell-by date because you feel obliged to keep it going or are nostalgic about the past. It's ok to outgrow friendships. As you evolve you are going to outgrow people that you *never* imagined yourself outgrowing. It is a natural part of life and sometimes friendships need to end because you know they are not good for you, and it hasn't worked for a long time. You can pour all the love, effort and energy you want into it, but it won't change the fact that it's finished. *So let go*, these things can't be forced. By letting go you make space for new friendships to come into your life. Ones that better match who you really are and can give you what you need.

HATERS ARE GONNA HATE

There will *always* be critics. There will *always* be someone who doesn't like you or what you are doing. There will *always* be someone who questions your ability or doubts your expertise. *That's just how it goes.* There will be people who will get mad over your success, your potential and your progress. *Let them be mad.* You are never going to please them all. So why bother trying to? The haters are gonna hate but know that it makes no difference to your world at all. You keep on doing you. You keep winning and thriving and living your best life. Because no matter what you do in life there is always going to be someone who doesn't like it, and you can't bring *your* party to a close for them. You've got to live your life on your terms and do what makes *you* happy regardless of what other people think. Insignificant people and their insignificant opinions of you are insignificant to your life. Remember that.

LET GO OF PEOPLE WHO ARE NOT YOUR PEOPLE

It's okay for you to outgrow people and it's ok for them to outgrow you too. At points, you will have to decide that it is no longer healthy for you to have them in your life and that you need to let certain people go in order to be happier and more at peace. How long have you spent imagining scenarios of them changing and things finally being different? Yet nothing has changed at all. They are who they are and no amount of your time and effort is going to change that. You have been in denial with yourself over the pain that they cause for long enough and maybe now your only option is to let them go. *You* can't heal in the same environment that hurt you. *You* can't grow if you are restricted by the people around you who keep you small. Letting go of people is hard, but there *will* be a day when you no longer want them. Let your focus be on people who match your future and not your past. Accept that some people are just not your people and the best thing you can do is let them go.

DON'T ACCEPT LESS FROM OTHERS

The truth is, sometimes people will treat you just well enough to keep you hanging on. They aren't completely horrible to you, but they aren't completely nice either. They feed you tiny crumbs of love and affection to keep you on the hook, but without ever giving you anything real. A constant routine of push and pull, they aren't prepared to love you right and they are too selfish to let you go. *How much longer are you going to let people like this take up space in your life? How much longer are you going to let them play with your emotions?* You know you deserve better than this, but you will only get better if you change who you let into your life. You set the standard for how people treat you by what you are willing to accept from them. They will *never* change, but *you*, you can break out of this loop. Set the standard *higher* and decide that you are going to be firm with who you invite into your life. Remember it's a *privilege* to be in your life, you get to invite or decline anyone's presence in your world. Be choosy and only let in people who are willing to give you everything that you deserve.

WHAT'S IN IT FOR YOU?

Make sure you are getting a good deal out of it too. I know you are so kind and so giving to everyone, but don't forget to look after yourself too. Don't let anyone walk over you. Don't let anyone forget that your needs matter too. Make yourself a priority, because you are. Make sure that you are happy with the outcome – don't be afraid of fighting your corner. So ask yourself, what's in it for you?

CHOOSE PEOPLE WHO CHOOSE YOU

Never forget that it is a *privilege* for people to be part of your life. Not everyone currently in your life deserves to be there. You have to ask yourself, *'Are the people I am choosing to prioritize actually choosing to prioritize me too?'*. You have the power to decide who you spend time with, who gets to take up space in your thoughts and who gets to receive what you have to give. *So be selective* about who you let into your life. Choose the people who choose you. Because when you do this *everything* changes. Choose the people who genuinely care, the people who see your worth and who want great things for you. Choose the people who make you happy and who bring you peace. Choose the people who value you, those who put the effort in and consider you important. The ones who are always rooting for you and who *love* to see you win. The people who love you as much on your worst day as your best day. *Choose those people*, the people who expect nothing from you in return for their love and fully accept you as you are. These are the people who change your life for the better. So *choose them* and skip the rest.

PEP TALKS FOR INNER PEACE

TAKE A DEEP BREATH

Relax your shoulders, loosen your jaw, unclench your teeth and roll the tension out of your neck. Now, uncurl your fingers, unscrunch your eyebrows and shake your body out. Sit perfectly still for just a moment and take a deep, energizing breath. Fill up your lungs completely, and then exhale out all of that tension. *Let it all go.* You need to give yourself a break, the pressure you put on yourself is immense but also, *it's not necessary.* You do not need to carry the weight of the world on your shoulders, it is not all yours to carry. You are allowed to switch off and not worry about everything for just a moment. I promise, the world will keep spinning even if you take a pause. So, right now, just take a moment to escape the chaos and *just be.*

DEAR OVERTHINKER

Dear overthinker, you are doing it again. You are *exhausting* yourself with mental gymnastics. Maybe it's time to give your brain a breather and *slow it all down.* Instead of going round and round in your mind, understand that you cannot solve it all and that honestly it's going to be ok regardless of whether you worry about it or not. *So don't.* Remind yourself that actually you *don't* need all the answers right now and that not everything needs to be thought about in that much depth. Remember that you are not supposed to have a perfectly engineered plan covering every possible scenario and that things *will* still work out ok if you just take life one day at a time. So *let go* of all the heavy thoughts because it is all going to work out just fine for you. Focus only on what you *can* control and make peace with the things that you can't. Know that life is *always* working in your favor so it's ok for you to relax a little.

TURN THE PRESSURE DOWN

Please don't be so hard on yourself, nothing matters as much as you think it does. Nothing is ever life or death. You need to turn the pressure down on yourself and take a moment to realize that it is all going to be ok and you are going to be *fine*. Whatever it is you are facing, it is *not* the end of the world. You need to take the pressure off of yourself and not be so hard on yourself for not knowing all the answers. You will figure this out just like you have always done. If you take a step back, shrink it down and look at it from a different perspective then you are going to get where you want to go a lot faster. Things often do not matter as much as we think they do, we let them feel much bigger than they really are. Don't lose sight of what actually matters, *your happiness*. This doesn't matter enough to steal your peace. Give yourself a break and turn the pressure down, it is all going to be ok.

YOU GET TO DECIDE

You get to decide how your life looks. You get to decide how to spend your time on this planet, where you work, what you do, who you are with and who you become. Make sure you are living for *you* and not for other people. Live your life in a way that pleases *you*. It is ok to let other people's expectations of you down, but it is not ok to let yourself down. Don't be scared to say no, to enforce a boundary, to tell people that their ideas for you don't work for you. Be brave enough to dictate what you want for your life. Stop giving away your power by letting other people decide what *your* life should look like. Because the choice is *always* yours. You get to decide what's next for you, you get to decide how much you achieve and what is enough for your life. You get to decide what really matters to you, *you are your north star.*

MAKE PEACE WITH NOT KNOWING ALL THE ANSWERS

Sometimes you need to make peace with not knowing all the answers; not knowing why it happened, or who caused it, or if it could have been different. The truth is you aren't always going to get the answers you need and sometimes you are going to be left with unknowns. Please don't waste your time and energy searching for answers that you will not find. Not everything *has* an answer and not everything is made to be known. You may never know why they treated you like they did. You may never know if they still think about you or regret what happened. You may never know why it had to be the way that it was. You have to make peace with the fact that you will never get the answers you want. Hunting for answers that can't be found is a waste of *your* time, energy and inner peace and keeps *you* stuck in that loop. If you are honest with yourself; you know that the why, what and how don't really matter anymore. It's been and gone. What has happened has happened and what is done is done. What matters now is that you move forward. Moving forward means leaving some questions in the past so that they do not steal your future happiness. The truth is you can move on and be happy with your life *without* knowing everything because the only thing you *need* to know about it all is that it is behind you now.

LET YOURSELF REST

I know you are tired, and I know you are working *so hard* to build yourself the best life possible. But I also need you to know that it's ok to rest for a moment. Being 'on' all of the time is not sustainable. You are exhausted because you are overthinking everything. But that's exactly it, you are *over* thinking. You are fixating and worrying about things that are ultimately going to be ok whether you worry about them or not. You are allowed *worry-free* moments. You *can* take a minute to relax without it all falling apart. Take a mental breather and let yourself *under* think for once. Let yourself realize that not everything needs your constant management and care. Your life is in a better position than you realize and if you would just stop and *rest* for a moment, I think you would see that too.

SAY 'NO' MORE

No, thank you. Thank you, but *No*. That sounds great but I won't be able to make it. I will pass on this thanks. *NO*. That doesn't work for me. Decline. However you choose to say it, start saying '*No*' more. It's not as hard as you think it is. You can't control everything in life, but you *can* control what you agree to. Don't be afraid to opt out of the things that don't work for *you* and feel good about doing so. The word *No* is enough. You don't need to explain it, you don't need to justify it. *No* is sufficient. *No* is the most liberating word in the dictionary. You get to remove yourself from all the things that you don't want to do with a simple two-letter word, and you don't have to feel guilty about doing so. You aren't doing anything wrong by protecting your own happiness and doing what is best for you. Stay authentic to yourself. Everything you do is a use of *your* energy, *your* time, *your* resources and *your* life. So you've got to spend these things wisely. You can't pull yourself in a thousand different directions just to keep everyone else happy. The world won't end just because you politely declined something. The word '*No*' makes a big difference - use it.

YOU DO NOT NEED TO CARRY EVERYTHING

This is your reminder that the weight of the world is not *yours* to carry. I know that you are stronger than most people, but please remember that you *have* to pick and choose what you carry. You cannot carry it all, it's way too much. You are going to have to put some of it down, let some of it go and trust that it will *all* be ok. Share the load, let someone else carry some of the burden with you. After all, it was never down to you to carry it *all* in the first place. You are a problem solver and that's why you are taking all of this on, but you need to remember that not every problem is *yours* to solve. Some challenges are not for you to fix, they belong to others, and it is up to them to step up. All the little things that you are worried won't work out, *will* work out, life has a plan for you and that plan *always* works out. So take a breather, have a moment for yourself where you just let it *all* go. You will only realize just how heavy all the things you have been carrying are when you let yourself put a few things down.

YOUR LIFE IS FULL OF CHAPTERS

Your life is made up of chapters. Some chapters are there to grow you. Some to soothe you. Some to make you realize how loved you are. Some to test you. Some to teach you how to be tougher. Some to remind you to be softer. Some to push you. Some to help you learn who you really are. But the thing all chapters have in common is that they are temporary. Each chapter of your life will come to an end so that a new one can begin. No chapter can last forever. Which means this: If you are going through a particularly tough chapter right now then know that it will one day be over. It can't last forever; it will end and you can move on from this. Equally, if you are in a magical chapter of your life then let yourself slow down and enjoy it. Savor the moment that life is giving you and enjoy it *right now*. Don't waste a single second of it. Make the most of it and be grateful that you got to experience it. Each chapter in your life is there for a reason. It's going to shape you and grow you. It takes you through experiences that you need to have in order to become the best version of yourself. But whatever chapter you are in, know that it serves a purpose and is building you in some way.

IT'S NOT YOUR PROBLEM

Start telling yourself *'It's not my problem'*. Because it really isn't. You do not need to get involved with everything and not everything is *your* issue to solve. Protect your peace by reminding yourself that you do not need to fix everything for everyone else. You have your own life to focus on, so get comfortable with letting *other people's* problems be *other people's* problems. You can't keep saving everyone, at some point they need to learn to save themselves. Opt out of headaches that you don't need to take on. Know when to walk away. Let someone else deal with it because it simply isn't *your* problem. You protect your peace and your sanity when you realize that some things have absolutely *nothing* to do with you.

YOU DON'T HAVE TO BE STRONG ALL THE TIME

You don't have to be strong all the time. Cry, let off some steam, have a moment where you let it all go and let yourself feel what you need to feel. You are still a strong and resilient person *even if* you give yourself a moment to drop your guard and have a break from being so put together all the time. It's ok to put down what you are carrying and regroup for a moment. You don't have to be strong all the time.

REBUILD YOURSELF

Never forget that you can rebuild yourself back up from anything, *including* rock bottom. You are fully capable of rising up from the darkest of moments and in doing so you can change the course of your entire life. So many people fear finding themselves at rock bottom. But we forget that rock bottom gives us a unique opportunity to become whoever we want to be. It is a clean slate to rebuild yourself exactly how you want to. You can build the most determined, strong-minded and breathtaking version of yourself. You can take every mistake you have ever made, every challenge you have faced, every ounce of pain and hurt you have endured and use that to build the most amazing version of yourself. Magnificent people are not born, they are built through the challenges that they have faced. It is a *privilege* to have faced the challenges you have faced - yes it hurt, but it also *transformed* you into something you could never have become otherwise. You are stronger, smarter and more capable *because of it*.

YOU DON'T ALWAYS HAVE TO KEEP THE PEACE

The path of least resistance is very appealing, sometimes it seems so much easier to just go with the flow and keep the peace. But in keeping everyone else happy, the person who has to sacrifice their happiness is often *you*. Sometimes to get actual peace in your life, you need to stop trying to please everyone else and take a stand against things that really don't work for *you*. Boundaries are a good thing, standing up for yourself is a good thing, and defending yourself is a good thing. If something doesn't work for you, *say so*. Push back, say no, shake things up, start a riot if you have to. These are all forms of self-care and will do you *a world* of good. You do not always have to keep the peace, nor do you have to keep everyone else happy. You have got to protect yourself and sometimes that involves causing a little chaos.

THE GOAL

The goal is not the job, the house, the achievements. The goal is not the reputation, the weight loss, or the money. The goal is not the things that matter far less than you think they do. The goal is to be happy with yourself and your life. The goal is to get better every day, to be healthier, happier, more at peace and more fulfilled with your life. The goal is to like yourself, appreciate yourself and respect yourself, *that's* the goal.

IF YOU ARE FEELING OVERWHELMED

If you are feeling overwhelmed, then I want you to know this: You do not need to deal with every little detail of your life *right now*. Not everything needs to be dealt with in *this* present moment. Things can wait, your world is not going to come crashing down if you put things aside and let yourself just have this moment to come down and breathe. If you are feeling overwhelmed, please be kind to yourself and realize that not everything is as important or urgent as you think it is, it just *feels* like a lot when you are anxious. You can't control everything in life, what will be will be, but you *will* make it work. You have *always* made it work. Remember *nothing* is ever the end of the world and *nothing* is ever do or die. So when it feels like it's all getting too big and overwhelming, shrink it back down and remember that the universe is always rooting for you and wants you to succeed. Remember, things can change quickly for the *better* and that they will *always* fall into place. You are absolutely fine.

LET GO OF WHAT DOESN'T SERVE YOU

Sometimes you need a deep clear out. Not of your possessions but a clear out of the things that take up space in your mind, heart and soul. When your home is cluttered, you have a declutter. You get rid of the things that represent old versions of you or that you don't need anymore. But emotionally, we rarely do this and instead carry around things for much longer than it is beneficial. Painful memories, past hurt, regret, insecurities, old limiting beliefs, embarrassing memories, old fears - things that really don't add any value but take up *so much* space. Isn't it time to let it all go? You hold on to these things because you haven't yet realized that it is completely ok for you to let it all go. Know that you are free to move on and leave it all behind you. You do not need to hold onto *anything* that steals your peace or prevents your happiness. Give yourself permission to let go and be free.

NOTHING IS MORE IMPORTANT THAN PROTECTING YOUR INNER PEACE

Above all, protect your peace and do not sacrifice your inner peace for *anything*. We are all guilty of letting things seem bigger than they are. Problems will always appear, but problems *can always* be solved. These things are not worth losing your peace over. Life is so much more simple than we let ourselves think, sometimes we give too much power to things that don't matter as much as we think they do. If it causes chaos in your life then you don't need it, take action to remove it. Remember that you get to choose what takes up space in your life and what doesn't. Choose things that enhance your inner peace, and if it's not life or death then don't sweat over it. Nothing is as precious as your inner peace, and it is your job to protect it.

STRESS LESS

If you look back, was anything you once worried so much about ever as urgent or as important as you thought it was at the time? Likely, the answer is no. You stress yourself out and worry about things *far* more than you need to. In hindsight you can see that it was never worth losing so much of your peace over and yet you got so worked up about it at the time. Promise yourself that going forward you are not going to let yourself sweat the small stuff and you are going to be really selective over what you let bother you. Promise to always choose to see things in a better light and reframe the situation for a better perspective. Promise to not take life too seriously and be reassured that most things are easily fixed and are not worth losing your peace over. Most of the things we stress about never end up as bad as we imagine and aren't worth wasting our precious peace over. Remember that stressing about something rarely makes it any better and know that whatever it is that's bothering you right now, is going to be ok in the end. It always is.

PEP TALKS TO HELP YOU HEAL

YOU WILL HEAL

Give yourself time to heal and be patient with yourself as you do so. Every single day you are making progress on your healing journey. Even when it feels slow and hard, trust that you *are* moving forward. It will get better, and you *are* healing, you just need to trust the process. No pain or struggle lasts forever, including what you are going through now. But here's the thing about healing, sometimes it has to feel worse before it gets better. To heal you *need* to feel. You need to let yourself sit in *all of it* in order to work through it. That part is the hardest. That's the part when it feels all too much. However, there will be a day when your life looks totally different, and this is all behind you. That is what you are doing this for. Nothing happens by accident, even your darkest days are there to lead you to somewhere better.

FORGIVE YOURSELF

Whatever parts of your journey that cause you to carry regret, it's time to let go, move on and *forgive yourself*. Maybe what you really need is to wipe the slate clean, shed all the baggage you have been carrying and move forward with a fresh start. *Forgive yourself* for your mistakes. *Forgive yourself* for your wrong decisions, for acting on impulse, for missing opportunities. *Forgive yourself* for choosing the wrong people. For hurting others and for hurting yourself. *Forgive yourself* for staying in places longer than you should have. For not demanding what you are worth and for accepting less than you deserve. Throughout everything, you did the best you could at the time and that was good enough. You are human, you are allowed to get it wrong sometimes, it's part of the journey and part of growth. But equally know that you are allowed to *forgive yourself* and put your past behind you. The experience of life is imperfect, which means *we are imperfect*. We are all going to mess up and when we do we are not imprisoned by those mistakes for the rest of our lives. It's time to forgive and let it go.

DEAL WITH WHAT YOU NEED TO DEAL WITH

You have to deal with what you need to deal with otherwise it's always going to hold you back. Even though it's hard, you must do the work to overcome your doubts, insecurities and traumas otherwise they will *always* have power over you. Do the work and deal with what you need to deal with so that you can learn to love yourself, understand yourself and rebuild yourself once and for all. If you don't heal what you need to heal it doesn't go away. It may be the hardest thing you ever have to do, but you can't keep sweeping your demons under the rug. It's going to be an uncomfortable and ugly process, but once you've wrestled with each of your challenges and taken away their power, a new way of life can begin. One full of confidence, fulfilment, stability, inner peace and happiness. So many people build a life that looks good on the outside but deep inside things are actually very unstable. Don't let that be you, deal with what you need to deal with.

LET GO OF THE PAST

You carry so much around from your past that you don't need to. Past relationships, past mistakes, past versions of you, past rejections, past fears, past doubts. What would happen if you were to just let it all go? Yes, all of that mattered at the time, but that was *then,* and this is *now.* You are in a new chapter now, your life is different now and you have every right to let it all go and start again. Your past doesn't define you, it doesn't own you and it doesn't dictate your future. Your life is amazing now. It's time you let yourself wipe the slate clean, start over and allow yourself to begin again. It's time to let go.

YOU ARE GROWING

I know you may not be exactly where you want to be right now but you *are* growing and it is beautiful. You have grown so much already and learned so much about who you are. You have discovered your strength and taken the time to really understand who you are and what you deserve. You have learnt how to love yourself even though it has been hard sometimes. You figured out what you like, what you don't like, and you have started to apply that to your life. You know how worthy you are and how beautiful and magical your soul is. You are learning to love your body for all of its imperfections. *You have come so far.* You have overcome your fears, crushed your doubts and learnt how to stand up for yourself. You have learnt how to enjoy things again, how to feel free and how to embrace the constant changes in life. Your journey has been *incredible* so far, and you aren't done yet.

LET YOURSELF ENJOY THE SLOWER SEASONS

Life comes in seasons. There are going to be fast seasons where everything flourishes at a rapid pace and there are also going to be slower seasons. Let yourself *enjoy* the slower seasons. Often, we fear that these slower seasons are time wasted, whereas actually slower seasons are *vital* to your success. It's in these slower times where you digest your hard work, process things and recharge. Embrace the slower seasons by sinking into whatever feels good in the moment. Drink tea in the stillness, read good books, enjoy walks in nature and *rest*. You need this down-time to grow, pause and recoup. You put immense amounts of pressure on yourself to always be achieving, performing and doing. But *you must* let yourself enjoy the slower seasons in your life too. *Indulge* in the slower seasons just as much if not *more* than the faster ones. We are not supposed to be productive all of the time, we are not supposed to be overachieving constantly, and we cannot expect our life to be one big upward trajectory. There needs to be slower seasons, which are still *incredibly* productive *just in a different way*.

PAUSE

Pause for a moment and let it all go. Just for one moment forget all of the things that take up so much space in your mind. *Pause* and realize that the world still spins if you take your foot off the gas and give yourself a chance to breathe. Sometimes it is only when you stop and pause do you realize that some things never warranted losing so much of your peace over the first place. Life is so stunningly beautiful when you slow down and focus on what actually matters. Sitting in peace doesn't mean you are sitting still. You are still moving forward and making progress in your life, but you are allowing yourself to enjoy the journey as you do. We make the mistake of thinking that pain means progress. That we need to be stressed in order to be moving forward - that is simply not the case. Peace goes well with progress too. You will get further feeling relaxed, at peace and happy than you will feeling overwhelmed.

MOVE ON TO BETTER THINGS

If it doesn't move you forward or if it doesn't match the person you want to be then it doesn't belong in your life. It is as simple as that. You can't expect your life to change for the better if you carry the same things with you that have held you back from getting there before. Give yourself permission to make changes to your life and *move on* to better things. Let yourself drop all of the deadweight and baggage that has been holding you back and allow yourself to actually live how *you* want to. You have to ask yourself - *Why am I still holding on to this? Is it actually good for me or is it just familiar?* Familiarity isn't always good, it is the same old same and will keep you in places that you have outgrown. This is about walking away from the things that no longer offer you what you need. It is you saying - *I can do better for myself and so that is exactly what I am going to do.* Always do what is best for you, even if that means shaking up your life and changing things completely. It's time for you to move on to better things.

NEVER LOOK BACK

As much as you have a past you need to remember that *most importantly*, you have a future. That future can be whatever you want it to be and only *you* get to decide what lies ahead of you. Your future is not dictated by your past and you are free to start over again whenever you need to, and it can be *completely* brand new. But *only* if you let yourself. Never look back, there is nothing there for you anymore. Let your future be your driving force because it is so, so bright.

GROWTH IS HARD BUT IT IS SO WORTH IT

What no one tells you about growth is that it's really hard. Any time you try to improve your life you are going to feel resistance. That is just how growth works. Growth requires you to outdo whatever you have done before and push yourself to expand, so actually, it makes perfect sense that growth is hard. There will be points on your growth journey when you will feel like you are not making any progress and that it's impossible to continue, but that doesn't mean magic isn't happening. It is. You *are* transforming your life for the better. The truth is, sometimes you need to break certain parts of your life in order to put it back together in a way that works *so* much better for you. It will get easier and easier as you go and when you come out the other side you will realize how everything you went through was worth it. You can do this, hang in there.

FIND OUT WHO YOU REALLY ARE

Who are you really? Who are you when you remove all of the layers that you have picked up on the way and mistaken for your identity? As you go through life you will have picked up so many pieces of baggage, beliefs, labels, opinions, and scars, as a result, you forget who you really are. Maybe it's time that you chip away at the layers that were never really you at all and rediscover yourself. You are not your past failings. You are not your job, or where you live. You are not your bad habits, and you are not your mistakes. You are not your past relationships, and you are not your fears or your traumas, but over time you have let these things define you and have made them your identity. You need to discover who you are without all of the noise that clouds your identity. You are so much more than you have let yourself realize. Peel back the layers and you will realize just how *incredible, worthy* and *wonderful* really are and always have been.

LET YOURSELF GROW

You're going to outgrow things along the way. Things that you could never imagine yourself outgrowing. Friends you thought you would have forever, romantic relationships that you were so sure would last, old versions of yourself and places that you once loved dearly. Outgrowing things that were once such a huge part of your life can be really scary. But you must realize that the things that once fit you are no longer compatible with who you have become. It is so tempting to hold yourself back, to resist the growth so that you can hold onto those things for a little longer. But there comes a point when you have to realize that there is nothing there for you there anymore. You have outgrown them and *that is ok*. You have to honor the growth that you have made and move on. You can't keep yourself small just to keep hold of things from your past. Let them go so that you can continue to grow. New growth will bring you so much more than holding onto the past will.

GO TO WAR WITH YOUR ANXIETY

You've got to go to war with your anxiety. You've got to fight back whenever it rears its head and claim back your peace. The more you push back against the voices of anxiety, the quieter they get. Anxiety can only grow if you feed it, and you feed it by believing the lies, worries and fears that it puts in front of you. As your anxiety creeps in, *question it* and hit back with facts. Remind yourself that your life is actually in a better place than your anxiety claims. You are safer than it claims, you are more loved and worthy than it claims, you are more capable than it claims and things are better than it claims. The first battle with your anxiety is the hardest, but it gets easier and easier the more you push back. Until one day, you realize that the voice of anxiety isn't so loud anymore, it's a small whisper that you can stamp out with a simple thought. You are stronger than your anxiety.

HISTORY IS NOT REPEATING ITSELF

There comes a point where you have to tell yourself that this time is different. That this is *not* the same person, *not* the same scenario and will *not* have the same outcome. You are *not* going to get hurt like you did last time. History is not repeating itself; this time *is* different and you have to let yourself enjoy it. If you let your fear of getting hurt again hold you back, then you are going to miss out on all the wonderful things that life has in store for you. You've got to believe that this time is different, that this is a new chapter of your life where things end *well* for you. Believe that this is the chapter where things work out for you, where you end up taking the winning prize, where it's your turn to get what you want. This chapter is new, it's *not* the same, it is a fresh start, and you have to recognize that things are different now for you. You are ok to relax and enjoy this, you are ok to drop your guard and soak it all up. History is not repeating itself, this time it is different, and things really have changed for the better.

STOP GASLIGHTING YOURSELF

Your experiences matter, your feelings, matter and your thoughts matter. Everything you have been through and everything you have dealt with is valid and matters. But in order to heal from this you are going to have to stop gaslighting yourself and denying your own feelings. Recognize your journey. Sit and process what you have been through and how deeply it made you feel. Don't discredit your story by refusing to acknowledge what you have faced. It was all real. So please, stop gaslighting yourself and instead let yourself process, feel, accept and heal.